PRAISE FOR *HUMANKIND*

"An elegant, wise book of love in action." **– DEEPAK CHOPRA**

"*HumanKind* has never been more timely." **–PEOPLE**

"The most uplifting and life-affirming book in years." **–FORBES**

"I believe we're all connected, and our purpose here on Earth is to help one another. In *HumanKind*, Brad Aronson shows us how to do this. The stories he shares will inspire you and, thanks to his practical tips, you'll feel empowered to act on that feeling and put kindness into action every day, in ways big and small."

–GABRIELLE BERNSTEIN, #1 *New York Times* bestselling author of *The Universe Has Your Back*

"If you need something to lift your spirits, get a hold of this book. It's the absolute best way to feel better about life."

–JANE GREEN, author of eighteen *New York Times* bestselling books

"Extraordinary stories." **–THE PHILADELPHIA INQUIRER**

"I can think of no better way to better yourself and the world than giving *HumanKind* a read."

–LORI DESCHENE, founder, Tiny Buddha

"*HumanKind* is filled with uplifting stories that will inspire you. Too often these days, the focus is on the negative, on disagreements and fights; this book is the exact opposite. It will make your day, every day you read it."

–MARK K. SHRIVER, President, Save the Children Action Network and author of *New York Times* bestseller *A Good Man*

"*HumanKind* is a celebration of the impact of small choices to transform ourselves and the world around us. It offers up an inspiring way for us to make the world better, even amid injustice, tragedy and misfortune. Read this book for inspiration and a path to the mindset and actions that will contribute to personal happiness and a world full of love."

–WENDY KOPP, founder, Teach For America

"*HumanKind* is a beautiful, sweet reminder of how the simplest act of kindness can have a profound and lasting impact on both the giver and receiver. It reinforces how compassion, empathy and goodwill are fundamental qualities the world needs now, more than ever."

–LAURA SCHROFF, #1 *New York Times* and internationally bestselling author of *An Invisible Thread*

"*HumanKind* is perfect for anyone feeling the weight of the world. It's a flashlight of inspiring stories and specific ways to help."

–NEIL PASRICHA, author of seven *New York Times* bestsellers including *The Book of Awesome*

"*HumanKind* will lift you up and open your heart. It left me feeling grateful and inspired."

–KEVIN KRUSE, *New York Times* bestselling author

"Thank you to Brad Aronson for spreading the gospel of kindness. This is a lovely and inspiring book on how we can make the world better with gestures big and small."

–A.J. JACOBS, author of numerous *New York Times* bestsellers including *Thanks a Thousand*

"Best books to read this year . . ." **–BELFAST LIVE**

HUMAN KIND

BRAD ARONSON

Cataloguing data available from Library and Archives Canada

ISBN 978-1-928055-63-1 (paperback)
ISBN 978-1-928055-64-8 (EPUB)
ISBN 978-1-928055-65-5 (PDF)

Cover and interior design: Morgan Krehbiel
Author photo: Andrew Sullivan

Published by LifeTree Media, an imprint of Wonderwell
www.wonderwell.press

Distributed in the US by Publishers Group West and in Canada by Publishers Group Canada

This book is dedicated to Mia and Jack.

. . . .

*One hundred percent of author royalties are
donated to Big Brothers Big Sisters.*

CONTENTS

INTRODUCTION

A FEW YEARS AGO, I attended the high school graduation of one of my mentees. All the students at Girard College (yes, that's actually the name of the high school) are there because of some sort of adversity in their lives. The vast majority of them are also from areas of Philadelphia where it's assumed that they won't go to college. In their neighborhoods, one in three kids drops out of high school and only a small fraction of those who do graduate continue their education.

At Girard, on the other hand, 100 percent of that year's graduates were accepted by colleges. These students beat the odds and went on to attend some of the best institutions in the country, including the University of Pennsylvania, Wesleyan and Howard.

At the graduation ceremony, parents who hadn't graduated high school were crying and cheering for their children who were. Children who were giving future generations a new standard to aspire to. I also met Girard alumni who have a lasting bond with their high school. The man sitting next to me was a seventysomething Columbia professor who had traveled from New York for the occasion, and he proudly belted out the school song along with the new graduates. He told me he's forever connected to Girard because of the impact the school had on his life.

Commencement speaker Marc Morial, president of the National Urban League, spoke passionately about the wonderful accomplishments of the students, and he talked about the world they'll inherit. He talked about the negativity that's so pervasive in the media. He questioned why a shooting in the neighborhood was more likely to be covered in the news than the annual success of this institution. By the time he was done, the same question was resounding in my head, and

I was hoping against hope to see a story about Girard's graduation in the news the next day.

But it wasn't to be. None of the news outlets said a word about it. Instead, I was informed of an arrest for shoplifting, an armed robbery and a car crash. Why did students who were beating the odds slip under the radar but a car crash and an arrest didn't? I'm not sure, but writing this book is my effort to share more of the stories that matter.

When my wife was sick with leukemia, we spent a lot of time at the hospital, and a patient advocate suggested we create projects to give us purpose and focus during such an emotionally draining experience. So I began writing about the friends, family members and complete strangers who rescued us from that dark time, often with the smallest gestures, and I found that I didn't want to stop. I knew that like Girard College, the world was full of other people's inspiring stories that didn't make the news, so I sought them out. I scoured the Internet, I talked to people at countless nonprofits and I asked everyone I knew for their stories. And I found what I was looking for.

I found the story of the third-grade teacher who changed a boy's life with a simple lesson in shoe-tying. The story about the band of seamstress grandmothers who descend on Philadelphia every week to patch clothes—and, in the process, mend hearts—for homeless people. The story of the woman whose decision to make an extra meal to feed someone in need led to a movement that's provided more than sixteen million meals. And so many more about people whose love for others has made a difference in the world.

The heroes in *HumanKind* don't command an army of helpers or have an abundance of free time. They're everyday people who focus on what they can do to make a difference. Their acts of kindness change lives and even save them. These everyday heroes don't just hope the world will get better—they make it better.

Each chapter's conclusion and the Hall of Fame at the end of the book highlight easy ways you can have a meaningful impact. You'll discover where a $195 donation can cure someone's blindness and where $500 can pay for a treatment that enables a disabled child to walk. You'll find a dozen ideas, many of which surprised me, that people going through difficult times suggest as the best ways to help them. You'll discover thirteen nonprofits that will forward your letters of encouragement to hospitalized kids, foster youths, recently diagnosed cancer patients, deployed troops and others who will cherish your support. You'll see how buying someone a meal or sharing a few words of encouragement at the right time really can change a life.

I hope *HumanKind* leaves you feeling grateful for the blessings in your own life. I hope the people you read about also leave you feeling inspired and plant the seeds for more inspiring stories. Stories about the difference *you* decide to make in the world.

CHAPTER

1

....

LOVE DOES

"Every day I wake up and say, 'I'm going to save a life.'
All day long I look for situations where I can save a life. And I
do it. Every day I save at least one life. Today I probably saved
five lives. And I feel good about it. Try it. Wake up tomorrow and
say, 'I'm going to save at least one life today.' Even helping an
old woman across the street counts. Even responding to an email
and helping someone make an important decision saves a life.
Even reaching out to a distant friend and asking, 'How are you
doing?' can save their life. You can save a life today. Don't let the
sun set without doing that. You are Superman."
—JAMES ALTUCHER

"MIA HAS LEUKEMIA."

What?

"It's important for her to start treatment immediately," the
oncologist said. "She'll need to be admitted to the hospital as soon as
possible."

Is this really happening? To us?

The doctor kept talking, and despite the chaos happening in my
head, I paid attention as best I could and took notes. But it wasn't
till we left her office and I looked back over what I'd written that it

started making sense to me: "Don't read about leukemia online . . . . The treatment is two and a half years, so focus on one step at a time and not the entire process . . . . Mia's odds are very good . . . . A new treatment regimen had clinical trial results with a high level of success, and Mia will receive that treatment . . . ."

One thing I very clearly remembered hearing was that Mia would undergo a month of inpatient chemotherapy—which would encompass Christmas and New Year's—followed by nine months of intense outpatient chemo, during which my wife would probably feel awful. And *that* would be followed by about a year and a half of maintenance chemo.

It *was* really happening. It was going to be a rough two and a half years.

Right off the bat, things were going to change drastically at home. Mia was typically in charge of anything resembling work around the house, while I served mainly as chief fun officer. I was the one to persuade Mia and our five-year-old son, Jack, to dance outside in the rain, the one to invent new sloppy desserts, and the one to come up with indoor games that were a little reckless and usually ended with something in pieces on the floor. Now I would have to perform the duties of director of fun, household operations manager *and* defender of normalcy. Social workers told us that because of Jack's young age he wouldn't become anxious or even detect that Mom was less involved as long as I managed everything Mia used to do and remained upbeat. If his life didn't change, he wouldn't notice. No pressure.

I was determined not to blow it, but I was also terrified and completely unprepared. Before long I was exhausted, too. I couldn't even think clearly enough to delegate when people reached out to help. Wearily, I told them I'd get back to them. Fortunately, they knew better than to wait for me. Instead, family and friends took the initiative to make our lives easier in more ways than I knew were possible.

My brother, Rob, and his wife, Tippi, talked to nurses, doctors, and cancer patients and made a comprehensive list of items that people undergoing inpatient chemotherapy need. Then they went out and bought every single item on the list and dropped off the mountain of stuff just before Mia was admitted. There were special pillowcases to keep her scalp from getting irritated when her hair fell out, lemon drops to take away the chemo aftertaste, special mouthwash to ease the pain of mouth sores, creams for the skin irritation chemo would cause—the list went on and on. Rob and Tippi had even thought to include some books on explaining cancer to a child.

My cousin Betsy came by our house one day with an enormous bowl of candy for me to give to the nurses who took care of Mia. Betsy knew my high opinion of them, and she also knew I might not find the time to pick something up.

My colleague Mitchell, a fellow board member of a local non-profit, knew I wouldn't be able to pay as much attention to my non-profit commitments and basically said, "Here's the work I'm going to do for you, and I want to do more. What else can I do?" I wouldn't have asked for help even though I needed it (a problem I've since overcome), but Mitchell made it easy to accept assistance.

Mia's friend Meg came to visit almost every week. She brought lunch, planned a weekly craft project, and brought all the supplies for each project. Meg's family and work life is so busy that it's hard for us to schedule a night to go out together, but when Mia needed her, Meg wouldn't let anything get in the way of being there.

My cousin Katy and her husband, Jason, who work full time and have four young kids, often told us how easy it would be for them to add Jack to their pack. They were happy to take him on vacations or entertain him for weekends or any time we needed.

When spring came around, Mia's friend Dawn emailed me: "I know Mia usually takes care of Little League sign-ups, so I thought I'd let you know that sign-up is due this week if Jack wants to partic-ipate. Let me know your preferences and I'll help with this." She also ensured that Jack was put on a team with a family that could help us with transportation since we didn't know how available I would be to drive. This was despite a reasonable league policy against requesting specific friends for teams.

At one point, Mia started craving processed cheese products as a side effect of chemo, and when our friend Jon visited from Boston, he came bearing bags of Cheez Doodles, jalapeño-flavored Combos and packages of freakishly shaped and vividly colored products I'd never even heard of (and we both hope never to taste again). It was a welcome surprise, injecting some pleasure into what would otherwise have been another monotonous day of treatment. Jon ended up visiting regularly, even when we told him it wasn't necessary, and he never made it sound as if the trip from Boston to Philadelphia had been anything but a breeze.

At another point, Mia expressed concern about losing her eyebrows and eyelashes. She was fine with losing her hair, but this was a different thing altogether—you can't hide missing eyebrows and eyelashes with a wig. When my cousin Andrea heard this, she took it upon herself to exhaustively research the market and send a large box filled with things like eyebrow pencils, markers, gels, powders, brushes, liners and shapers. There was also a product called Lashes to Die For, which gave us a good therapeutic laugh. (We guessed the manufacturer doesn't typically market to cancer patients.)

And then there were our parents. When they asked how they could help, I never knew what to ask for and put them off. Of course, most parents aren't big on being put off, and ours would simply arrive in Philadelphia from Seattle and New Jersey bearing the gift of their time. They'd stay as long as several weeks and entertain Jack, cook, do laundry, and stay positive.

We also had a long list of friends and family members who would pick up Jack after school when I was at the hospital or at chemotherapy with Mia. Not a single one ever mentioned any logistical challenges they may have faced. Instead, they all told us how happy they were that we'd asked and that they could help.

And amid it all—amid the nonstop comings and goings, the trips to the hospital, and the increasingly challenging task of preserving normalcy—I checked the mailbox one day and found a Ziploc full of packages of something called Wikki Stix. On the bag, our neighbors had written, "We love making things as a family. See what you think! XO." I took the bag inside, and Jack and I promptly proceeded to connect the wax-coated yarn to make cars, spaceships, and anything else we had the urge to create. It was a blast, a much-needed port in the storm.

That isn't the half of it. Not even close. So many people did so much for us that I hesitated to mention *any* of them here because I'd have to leave out far more than I could include. Their gestures ran the gamut from simple notes of support sent by people we barely knew, to meals dropped off by friends, to my cousin Dave's offer to move into our house and help keep things going during Mia's treatment. Here's the email he wrote me:

Brad,

I'm sorry to hear the news but Davida has told me this is very beatable and you are with the BEST doctor. If you feel you need a second opinion I'm happy to call relationships in New York as well.

In the meantime, please, please, PLEASE use me. I have done some thinking and I'm the willing and logical choice to be your first call for every little errand or Jack-related need.

Firstly, my job is super easy and requires very little of my time, which can be covered by my dad or one of our workers anyway, so I can be ready at a moment's notice or for regular events like picking up Jack at school or tennis.

Secondly, I'm local. I am in Philly every weekday and Davida and I discussed it and she wouldn't mind (in fact she suggested it) if I moved to Philly for the month Mia is in the hospital. I would be at my parents' place, so I'm very convenient and could be there for Jack full time if necessary. I could even stay over for a night or a month if you need an overnight sitter.

Thirdly, I'm the logical choice. I have no important responsibilities.

- *Richard is a single dad and low man on the totem pole at work.*
- *My sister Betsy has Charlotte, is pregnant, and also helps my mom.*
- *My dad is focused on my mom and building the house for her.*
- *My sister Katy has four kids and lives far away.*
- *Rob and Tippi live far away as well as have their own kids.*

Fourthly, I'm responsible. I can be relied on and I follow directions exactly to the letter. You or Mia can write out anything you want done and know I'll follow it out exactly as it's written (even grocery shopping or cooking for Jack . . . I follow recipes very well). I may not have refined parenting skills yet, but I can certainly step in and follow your orders well.

We love you and Mia, and both Davida and I are completely ready to help in any way possible.

Best,
David

We didn't take him up on his offer to move in, but we did recruit him for Jack's team of chauffeurs.

Dave's email sums up the no-stone-unturned approach that the people in our lives took to our situation. They anticipated every possible need of body and soul, and they all played a role in getting us through our all-consuming ordeal. Suddenly, our lives were full of slack—things that needed to be done that Mia and I didn't have time for—and friends, family, and veritable strangers picked up all of it. They saw every crack in our armor and rushed in to fill it, and looking back, the result reminds me of the Japanese tradition of filling cracks in pottery with gold, which produces something that's more beautiful than it was before it cracked. Others might not have been able to tell, but even though Mia was sick, we knew our lives were more beautiful because we'd received that love. In the end, we knew that even at the darkest moments, we'd never really been alone. And never will be.

There's never been a lack of opportunity to have that kind of effect in the world by helping others. Least of all now. Just look around—there are needs to be filled everywhere. In schools, in soup kitchens, in homeless shelters, in disaster zones. But if you do look around, you'll also see something else: all the people who are stepping up to pick up the slack. Yes, it can be paralyzing to think about the level of need out there, but if we do what we can, that will be enough. No expression of love is wasted, and even the smallest gestures tend to go much further than we think they will.

Remember how far Jon's gift of junk food went. It didn't cost him much time or money to pick it up at a grocery store, but the thought he put into it—the effort to empathize—meant everything to us. When it comes to caring for others, don't underestimate the power of the most modest investment. There's nothing modest about the results.

A VILLAGE TURNS OUT

There really is strength in numbers. The concept is sort of like a patchwork quilt made by many hands. Each person provides a single patch, and when the pieces are assembled they add up to something capable of providing comfort and protection. Stephanie Welter witnessed this phenomenon when her community came together on behalf of her son, Joe, who has autism.

When Joe gets upset, he hurts himself. He'll slam his head against the floor, a brick wall, a door, or anything else that's nearby. "I can't describe how terrible it is to fear that your seven-year-old child will hurt himself and to see it happen before you can stop it," Stephanie says. "Joe also runs away from us when we're not looking, and my husband and I are always fearful that if we turn around to do something as simple as getting his baby sister out of the car, he might disappear and get hurt."

Breaking with routine also brings the risk of "complete meltdown" and injury, Stephanie says. "So we don't. And that keeps us from going out socially with other families, which would often leave me feeling like we were going through this alone."

For Joe, getting older resulted in further social isolation. When he was younger, he could play with kids his age, but more recently he's had trouble dealing with loud noises, and his abilities don't align with other kids'. It's also hard for him to play with others when his play amounts to lining up twenty Matchbox cars in a specific order and making sure none of them are moved, which would result in a meltdown.

The Welters want Joe to have a future, to live a full life and be as independent as possible. So when they learned that an organization called 4 Paws for Ability provides autism service dogs that help people with the same types of problems Joe has, they were thrilled. The dogs are trained to track kids with special needs when they run off, to recognize when the kids are getting irritated and to calm them down before they can hurt themselves. The service dogs also serve as a social bridge to other children.

And then the Welters learned that, given the expense of training a service dog, 4 Paws required families to contribute $15,000 at the time, which is only a small portion of the total cost. The Welters figured that even with help from friends and family, it would probably take them a year and a half to scrape together that amount. But their son's future was on the line, and they knew what they had to do.

"Asking for help was almost as hard as opening up to our family and friends about Joe's situation in the first place," Stephanie says. "But our discomfort was less important than getting Joe the help he needed."

They began by including a letter with their Christmas cards explaining their goal. They made it clear that they didn't want to impose but that any amount would help. At the same time, the staff at 4 Paws worked with the local newspaper to run a story about Joe's situation. Two days after it was published, the Welters received a message on their answering machine: "I hope I have the right number. If you're the mom of Joe in the paper, my ladies' group wants to raise money for you."

"I had to replay the message four times," Stephanie says. "I was stunned. The group was from a church in the town where my son goes to school—people I didn't even know."

Later that week, Stephanie and her husband, John, were having breakfast when she got an email saying a company they'd never heard of had donated $2,000.

"I thought they'd added an extra zero by mistake," she says, still clearly moved by the gesture.

And the surprises kept coming. A hardware store donated $500. Stephanie's mother's accordion group donated money. High school students called the house to ask if they could do a fundraiser. A woman who worked at a restaurant called to say she'd persuaded her boss to donate 10 percent of their take on a particular day toward Joe's dog. When that day came, every one of Joe's teachers ordered food from the restaurant. His former speech therapist put together a gift basket to be raffled off for the occasion, and another family who had gotten a service dog through 4 Paws donated a bounce house to be raffled.

When Joe and his family went to the restaurant themselves that night, they saw his former preschool teacher for the first time in years, and Joe was so excited that he hugged her, stepped back and hugged her again—not his usual behavior.

"It was wonderful—we felt like celebrities," Stephanie says. "When we asked if the kitchen could make Joe a gluten-free grilled cheese with bread we'd brought, they said, 'Of course—he's the guest of honor.' There were so many people we knew there and many we didn't, and everyone came over to say hi."

In the end, the event raised $800 and brought the total to $15,000.

The Welters had put together lists of fundraising ideas to try, and they didn't need any of them. Thanks to the help of hundreds of people, most of whom donated under $20, they'd reached their goal in just three months.

"I'm so happy for Joe," Stephanie says. "Raising that money healed my heart, and I know now that we aren't isolated and alone. People we didn't even know sending in that $10 or $20 was life-altering for our whole family. We owe so much to everyone who helped us, and I will never forget it."

Since getting his goldendoodle, Mulder, Joe's life has changed radically. Like many children with autism, he hadn't slept well. He'd wake up after four hours and take hours to go back to sleep. Stephanie and John tried weighted blankets, aromatherapy, yoga, prescription medicine, melatonin and every other sleep aid they could find, but nothing worked until Mulder came along. The day he arrived, Joe finally got his first full night of sleep. And he's slept ten to twelve hours every night since then, which means the whole family has been able to sleep every night since then. Joe also hadn't been reaching the yearly educational goals his school set for him, but now he's achieving those goals. In fact, he achieved a year's worth within two months of Mulder's arrival, and for the first time, he's enrolled in a class with typical kids. Most important, Joe isn't known as the kid with autism. He's known as the kid with a dog, and as other children have met Mulder, they've gotten to know and appreciate Joe, too.

To give back, the Welters now also provide a home for Hercules, a 4 Paws breeding dog, and Stephanie and Hercules volunteer as a therapy team at the local ER, a cancer center, schools and anywhere else where there's a need. Stephanie also talks to most incoming 4 Paws volunteers so they hear firsthand the profound impact that Mulder has had on Joe's family.

THE SANTA BRIGADE

We can't foresee all the effects of an act of kindness. Sometimes we can't get past the idea that our contribution would amount to the proverbial drop in the bucket. But if no one ever got past drop-in-the-bucket thinking, hundreds of donors wouldn't have believed their $10 could make a difference to the Welters. We also wouldn't have organizations like Habitat for Humanity, the Salvation Army and Meals on Wheels. If Mary and Alice Goodwin and Elizabeth Hammersley hadn't seen the value in trying to develop the character of a group of "lost boys" in Hartford, Connecticut, in 1860, Boys & Girls Clubs of America wouldn't have seen the light of day. And if Larry Stewart hadn't met someone else in need during a time when he was just barely surviving himself, the Society of Secret Santas might not be putting black boots to the ground around the world every year.

When Larry was growing up in his grandparents' home in a small Mississippi town, he didn't know they were impoverished. It wasn't until he started school that he learned what he "lacked"—the bathrooms, telephones, hot water and gas stoves to be found in other kids' homes.

As a young adult, Larry confronted poverty again. Living paycheck to paycheck, he became homeless when his employer went out of business owing Larry more than one check. So Larry resorted to living in his car, covering himself in his laundry in an effort to stay warm and hoping to forget his hunger. By the time he'd gone two days without a regular meal, he was so desperate that he went to the Dixie Diner and ordered breakfast without knowing how he'd pay for it.

When he finished eating, he started looking around on the floor, pretending he'd lost his wallet. The cook even came out from behind the counter and helped him look.

Then, suddenly, the search was over.

"You must have dropped this," the cook said. He was holding a twenty-dollar bill.

Larry was so grateful that he made a vow to himself: as soon as he was able, he'd do something for others like what the cook had done for him. Over time, he became financially stable, and he set out to keep his vow. Although he wasn't well off by any means, he knew he couldn't put off getting started.

One evening, he stopped at a drive-in restaurant and noticed that the waitress was wearing a tattered coat that couldn't have been keeping her warm. When he handed her a twenty-dollar bill to pay for his food, he knew it was the moment.

"Keep the change," he said.

Tears welled in the waitress's eyes, and her hands shook as she held the money. "You have no idea what this means to me," she said, her voice shaking, too.

But Larry did have an idea what it meant to her.

Afterward, he was so inspired by what had happened that he started driving around looking for people who needed help. They weren't hard to find, and he gave away $200 in fives and tens.

The more successful Larry became, the more money he gave away. By the time he'd earned considerable wealth in cable and phone services in Kansas City, Missouri, he was anonymously giving away substantial amounts as a "Secret Santa." He consulted with local social workers, firefighters, and police officers to find needy and deserving recipients. He also found some of them on his own, at laundromats, social service agencies, government housing facilities, and businesses that paid minimum wage. At thrift stores, he often found people who were raising their grandchildren. When he would give them anywhere from $100 to $300, it would change the whole complexion of their Christmas as well as their outlook. For many of them, this money made it possible to buy presents and cover necessities like utility bills.

Larry didn't want people to have to beg, get in line or apply for money. "I was giving in a way that allowed them to keep their dignity," he said in an interview with a local news station years later. Just like the cook at the Dixie Diner had done for him.

All told, Larry gave away more than $1.4 million over the years. There are many stories from people whose homes he saved. People who told their families there wasn't going to be a Christmas but wound up being able to buy gifts because of the money Secret Santa gave them. People who were able to pay their bills and get their gas turned back on, thanks to Larry.

In 2006, after serving as an anonymous Santa for more than twenty years, Larry was diagnosed with terminal cancer. At that point, he decided to go public because a tabloid newspaper was about to reveal his identity. Larry thought he should be the one to tell his story, hoping it would recruit more Santas to take his place. He'd seen that every time a Secret Santa was written about in the media, the coverage was followed by a wave of new Secret Santa appearances. He hoped making his identity public would continue to add to the ranks.

Larry got his wish. Thousands of people visited his website and signed up to become Secret Santas. And based on the number of people who emailed the site about their experiences that Christmas season, the new Secret Santas did more than sign up; they also turned out in force.

When Larry died in 2007, his handpicked successor—an anonymous Kansas City businessman—took over for him and continues to lead the Society of Secret Santas today. Its members follow in Larry's footsteps around the world. The postings on the society's website tell of giving money to victims of fires, people who had been evicted from their homes, and veterans and military families in need. They tell of former NFL player Dick Butkus handing out hundred-dollar bills in San Diego and former Major League Baseball player Luis Gonzalez doing the same in Phoenix.

A foundation was also formed in Larry's honor to accept donations to be used by the Santas. The first donation was from former Kansas City parking attendant Sam Williams, who wanted to make a small gift in memory of the man who'd given him a hundred-dollar bill a few years before. "He gave me the biggest gift I ever got in my life," Williams told KMBC News.

Larry gave Secret Santas everywhere a gift, too. As the society's website says, "The compassion shared from one spontaneous random act of kindness is elevating, priceless and not easily explained. It is an instant connection between souls that can change a life forever. Being a Secret Santa has blessings beyond words."

What's more, it's a gift anybody can give. "It's not about the man, it's not about the money—it's about the message," says a Secret Santa. "Anyone can be a Secret Santa with a kind word, a gesture, a helping hand."

And what impact that gesture may have is anybody's guess. "You never know what one little act of kindness will do for somebody," as Larry told Ted Horn, chef-owner of the Dixie Diner, when he tracked him down twenty-eight years after their first meeting. "It can change their whole life. . . . It changed mine."[1]

SHERPA, MD

Larry said it—you never know. You never know which "drop in the bucket" will spark a movement, and you don't want to cheat the world out of that. But it's important to act regardless of the scope of the outcome. Even if an act of kindness helps just a single person for a single day, that's a gift. A gift I was fortunate enough to receive the day Mia was admitted to the hospital.

She started the day with surgery to insert a PICC line, a tube that ran from her arm near her biceps to a vein next to her heart to provide "express delivery" of chemotherapy medication and other drugs during her treatment. She was in pain afterward, and as I wheeled her to the room where she would live for a month, I saw how sick the other blood cancer patients were—the patients who'd already lost their hair and enormous amounts of weight and who had trouble walking because of their lack of strength and the IV poles that their PICC lines were tethered to. Although I kept it to myself, I was terrified.

Once Mia was in her room, I raced home to pack everything she'd need for the month, not wanting to leave her alone any longer than necessary. When I got back to the hospital, the parking spot I found was nowhere near the blood cancer department, so to save time I loaded myself up like a pack animal with the suitcase, the shoulder bags, the pillows and the trash bag filled with clothes so I could keep it to one long hike instead of two. Along the way, I was constantly dropping one bag or another because I couldn't get the right grip, and no matter how I adjusted the load, I couldn't find the right system. There *was* no right system—I was carrying too much. But I'd come too far to turn back—I'd already lost thirty minutes—so I didn't.

I was hard not to notice, but somehow an astonishing number of people passed right by. And I know they saw me because they commented to each other about how much that poor guy was carrying.

I'm generally calm, but this was a moment of hell within a day of hell, and I started clenching my teeth so hard it hurt.

This is what I get for trying to be a good person? For helping people whenever I can? Not a single person can help me with my bags???

Finally, just as I reached the point where I really didn't know what I'd do next, I heard the beautiful words: "You look like you need a hand. Can I help?"

I almost cried.

He was a young guy—a med student doing his residency, he told me—and he helped carry the load all the way to Mia's room. The detour might have cut his lunch break short or made him fifteen minutes late for a meeting—I don't know. I didn't even ask his name. All I know is that, years later, Mia's treatment is a blur in my mind but I vividly recall the stranger who took the time to help. Thanks to him, I made it through one of the most stressful days of my life, and I was that much more prepared for the next day's battle.

Life is a series of single days. If we make up our minds to help each other through those days, before we know it we'll be getting by. Of the many forms that love takes, maybe the most obvious one is a simple decision: a decision to put in the effort to make someone's life easier or more rewarding, even if just for a day. A commitment to doing more than hoping for the best for each other. It's bringing a homeless person a meal. It's being a positive influence for someone who needs one. It's helping in the wake of a disaster. It's taking some of the load off a guy whose legs are starting to buckle under the weight.

It's picking up the slack.

WHAT WE CAN DO

All of us can use a hand—we can't pick up all the slack ourselves. Whether we need help getting through a day, a year, or life itself, we all know what it's like to be in a position of need. Luckily, living is a team sport, and we all have it in us to provide an assist when someone's going through rough times, even if it's just to let them know we're thinking of them. Knowing that someone cares is often all we need to find the strength to keep going. That was the case when the parent of one of Jack's classmates sent us this note during Mia's treatment:

> Hi Mia,
> I just saw the notice to Primary B and wanted to say hello. It sounds from the note like your recovery has moved forward. But I just wanted to reach out to wish you strength and to let you know you have another person in your corner.
> Take care,
> Jill (mom of a 2nd grader)

We'd never met Jill, but her note had an unexpected effect on me. I felt energized, like something vital had been revived, and I have to believe it had something to do with the fact that Jill was a relative stranger. Love from our loved ones *and* strangers—it's pretty overwhelming.

Here are some things you can do to let others know you're thinking of them:

Do something small

We usually have a good idea of who could use some support, but we're often hesitant to do something. Maybe we don't know what to do, we think the person doesn't want the attention, we think we don't know them well enough, or we believe others have already reached out. Don't worry about any of that. When we let them know that we see them and we're thinking about them, it's appreciated. Beth Hackett, who lost her fifteen-year-old son, told Upworthy, "The most powerful communication of compassion and understanding was anonymous. Someone mailed us a gift card to the local grocery store: no name, no return address. . . . Weeks later when I pulled the gift card out of my wallet at the checkout, it was all I could do to hold back the tears."

Do something specific

We can ask, "What can I do for you?" or say, "Let me know if you need something," but when Mia was sick, I found it hard to even know what I needed. So it was wonderful when someone went ahead and did something without our asking. For example, neighbors shoveled our snow and friends dropped off meals. You can also make a specific offer: "Can I take your kids to the zoo one day this week after school? You might not need it this week, so take me up on it anytime. I'd love to do it." If you want to do more, you could add, "I'd also love to be given a job to do, so please reach out if one comes up."

Go all out

If you think something bigger would be welcome, go for it. We loved it when people went over the top. Here's a note Mia received from her crafting friends:

I just wanted to give you a heads-up that your craft ladies would like to cover you on the activity front—we are hatching a plan to create a variety of different craft kits for you to do in the hospital— and if company sounds appealing, the ladies and I would also love to make a visit early on to help craft and decorate. Carolyn has an elaborate idea about stenciling the windows. We could be your knitting circle on crack.

Think it over and let me know if that sounds appealing. If you don't want a home-decorating invasion, then you can just have the craft boxes, which will rock regardless.

The craft group wound up swooping in like the crew from *Queer Eye* to give Mia's hospital room a design makeover, which cheered her up and led to many enjoyable conversations with nurses who stopped by to check it out.

And our friends John and Kelly and their daughter, Fi, didn't just send Mia a care package—they sent her a fully decorated box crammed with stuff. More than we really needed yet exactly what we needed.

Schedule ongoing reminders

I'm convinced our friends Matt and Meg and my Aunt Leslie put recurring reminders on their calendars, because they reached out practically every week of Mia's treatment. Often, there's an outpouring of support soon after a diagnosis, a death, a divorce, or some other traumatic life event, but the support tends to taper off before too long. Meanwhile, the stress and the challenges continue, making check-ins over time greatly appreciated. And the support can be simple. Instead of asking about Mia's health, my Aunt Leslie sent a funny card every couple of weeks with a note about what was going on in her life. She didn't need to say anything else—we knew she was there for us.

Keep an eye out in your community

Kindness can extend beyond family and friends. Even if you hardly know someone, you can be a great source of support. When youth director Adeel Ahmad arrived at Nusrat Mosque in Coon Rapids, Minnesota, in February 2017—a time when hostility toward Muslims was growing in America—he found that someone had tied a large paper heart to the plants outside the door. Next to it was a pink envelope addressed to "Our Friends and Neighbors." Inside, the note read: "Dear Friends, Thank you for being here. You make all of us stronger, better and kinder. May peace be with us all."

Who can you send a note to?

Think like Santa

Give gifts to people you don't know. Let them know that someone out there cares about them even if they've never met you. In the *HumanKind* Hall of Fame at the end of this book, I've listed six organizations through which you can give gifts to kids who otherwise wouldn't receive any, to troops and to other people you don't know. (See page 204.)

....

I can't stress this enough: when someone is going through a crisis, emotions are magnified and even the smallest acts have tremendous power. Don't underestimate the strength you can provide with a two-minute gesture like a text, an email or a phone call.

. . . .

TAKE FIFTEEN MINUTES TO . . .

Who do you know who could use a lift? Write their names on a piece of paper or type them into your phone. How will you let them know you're thinking about them? You can send a text, a gift card, a book, or anything else you think they'd appreciate. If you don't have time to do something now, mark the dates on your calendar when you'll send your support to the people on your list.

. . . .

THE ROLE OF A LIFETIME

"Your life is an occasion. Rise to it."
—MR. MAGORIUM IN THE MOVIE
MR. MAGORIUM'S WONDER EMPORIUM

ONE DAY, my friend Tony and his five-year-old daughter, Maya, were driving through Northern California when she pointed to a woman standing on the sidewalk.

"Why is that lady standing on the corner with a sign?" she asked.

"She's homeless and asking for food," Tony said.

"Why don't we get her food?"

The question caught Tony off guard. Why *didn't* they get her food?

"I told Maya it was important to care about people, and I also thought of myself as a helper. Yet I was far from helping. So I did the only thing I could: I stopped the car and gave her my lunch."

Gaunt and bundled up under many layers, the woman gave him a big smile. "Thank you, and God bless you and your beautiful daughter."

"It had been in my face my entire life, so I grew not to see it," Tony says. "The problem seemed so vast that the question of how to make a difference seemed too complicated to solve. The easiest thing to do was not to respond. I feared that if I gave money, they might use it the wrong way. I had forgotten that they were people. It's so obvious, but I needed a five-year-old to show me that each homeless person is an individual. Maya knew that, and I needed to be reminded so I could be the person I wanted to be. I can't look past people because of my fears that they might not use the money the way they should. I need to at least make eye contact with people who are homeless and acknowledge them and see if I can do something to help."

Hearing Tony's story made me cringe as I thought about how often I'd passed by homeless people, often with Jack by my side, without even acknowledging them. I didn't want to be that person. I thought of myself as a helper and I've always told Jack how important it is to be kind, but Maya's question reinforced that no matter what we think or say, it's what we do that counts.

A MOTHER'S LESSON LIVES ON

Even a single action on a single day can set an example. In the case of former Philadelphia Mayor W. Wilson Goode Sr., the way his mother responded to an isolated situation when he was twelve years old influenced the homelessness program he established decades later.

When Goode was growing up on a tenant farm in North Carolina, a man knocked at the family's door at dusk one evening. "He said to my mother, who was cooking supper, 'I'm hungry,' and my mother, without hesitation, invited him in and shared our supper with him," Goode says.

"As a twelve-year-old at the time, I initially had an attitude about him eating up all of our supper. I was struck by the fact that she fed this man and did not even think about the fact that she had eight other people to feed and we had next to nothing."

But over the course of the meal, Wilson got over his "attitude" and felt his own stirrings of generosity. "I had saved about a dollar in nickels and pennies and dimes and had it stuck under my bed, and as he left I ran after him and said, 'Mr. Hobo,' and I gave him all the money I had in the world."

Three decades later, while Goode was serving as managing director for the city of Philadelphia in the early 1980s, he felt the same stirrings one evening when he got a call from the health commissioner, whose office was in the same building as his.

"Director, look at Love Park," the commissioner said.

Goode looked out his window at the park across the street. In the dusk, he could see that about fifty homeless men had taken up residence there. Recalling another encounter with homelessness that occurred in the dusk of a long-ago evening, he knew what he had to do.

Goode mobilized his team, and that same night they found a space in the basement of one of the city's firehouses, equipped it with cots and stocked it with food. Within a few hours, they'd created a temporary shelter and begun the city's first homeless program. Goode hadn't even taken the time to run the idea past the mayor.

"It came to my head because I needed to respond to a human condition that existed," he says. "After watching this man come and beg for food when I was twelve and watching my mother respond, I knew I had to respond to what I saw in front of me without hesitation."

Today, countless homeless people in Philadelphia have that single act of kindness by Goode's mother to thank for the help they've received. The city's comprehensive homeless assistance program grew significantly under Goode's administration and offers services that include homelessness prevention, emergency housing and a personal care home with residential care. Who knew that inviting someone to dinner could have such far-reaching effects?

MONDAYS WITH MAURICE

For Laura Schroff and Maurice Mazyck, a lunch at McDonald's was the meal that would make a dramatic impact on their lives. And it almost didn't happen.

"Excuse me, lady, do you have any spare change? I'm hungry," Maurice said on a September day in 1986.

Normally, Laura would have just kept walking. It was Manhattan, and it was easy to ignore people asking for money. "They were just so prevalent that most people simply looked the other way," she says in her inspiring book *An Invisible Thread*. "The problem seemed so vast, so endemic, that stopping to help a single panhandler could feel all but pointless. And so we swept past them every day, great waves of us going on with our lives and accepting that there was nothing we could really do to help."

And she did sweep past him. But then she stopped.

He said he was hungry.

She'd noticed he was young, but when she walked back to him, she saw that he was only a boy.

"Excuse me, lady, do you have any spare change? I'm hungry."

Laura didn't want to give him money and offered to take him to McDonald's instead. So the thirty-five-year-old advertising executive and the eleven-year-old panhandler in his dirty sweat suit and beat-up sneakers went to the Golden Arches for burgers, fries and chocolate shakes.

After lunch, Laura and Maurice walked through a nearby park, got ice cream and played some video games at an arcade. Then Laura gave him her business card and told him he could call if he needed anything. Over the next few days, she couldn't get him out of her mind, and when he didn't call, she realized he probably didn't have a quarter for a pay phone and went looking for him.

She found him close to the corner where they'd met. He said he'd been hoping she'd find him, so they went to McDonald's for burgers and fries again.

"Do you want to meet me on the corner next Monday night?" Laura asked as they ate. "I'll take you to the Hard Rock Cafe."

Maurice gave a big smile but hesitated. "Could I wear the clothes that I have on? They're the only clothes I own."

"Of course."

When he arrived Monday night, his face was sparkling clean and so were his burgundy sweats. He'd obviously gone all out for the occasion.

They went on to have a great time and decided to start meeting for dinner on Mondays on a regular basis—a tradition had been born.

It was a union of two worlds. Maurice lived in public housing in a one-room apartment filled with a rotating cast of relatives and drug addicts. It was a violent and chaotic home, and he was more or less responsible for himself. Meanwhile, two blocks away, Laura lived in a high-rise building that had a doorman—a true escape for Maurice in every way.

The first time he stepped into her world, though, there was tension on both sides. After about a half dozen get-togethers, Laura thought it was time to invite him for a home-cooked meal, but her friends told her it could be dangerous to allow a street kid into her home. As for Maurice, he couldn't have been more uncomfortable as he sat at the end of the couch, putting as much distance between them as possible. (Although Laura didn't know it at the time, he'd brought a box cutter he'd stolen because he thought there was some kind of catch to her generosity and he had no idea what it might be.) Wanting to clear the air and put them both at ease, Laura cut to the chase.

"The reason why I've invited you to my home is I consider you a friend, and friendship is built on trust. I want you to understand we're never going to have this conversation again, but if anything is ever missing from my apartment, we will no longer be friends."

Maurice looked mystified.

"Do you understand what I'm saying?"

"Miss Laura, you just want to be my friend? That's it?"

"Well, of course."

His face relaxed. "Miss Laura, a deal is a deal." Then he stood up and they shook on it.

During their weekly get-togethers, Laura and Maurice would have lunch, bake cookies, watch TV and read. Maurice would also take naps on Laura's couch and generally relish the chance to do what he wanted to do without anyone bothering him. It was a routine they both looked forward to, and it seemed to get Maurice through the week—until he showed up at Laura's apartment unexpectedly one Saturday. "I'm sorry to bother you, but I'm really hungry. Could we get something to eat?"

Laura fed him and learned that he hadn't had any food for two days. She also learned that this wasn't unusual—he often went without food. Sometimes he'd be so hungry that he felt like he'd been punched in the stomach.

Laura couldn't accept this and came up with a plan. "Look, Maurice, I can't bear the thought of you not eating every day, so this is what we can do: I can either give you some money for the week—and you'll have to be really careful how you spend it—or, if you prefer, on Monday nights we can go to the supermarket and I can buy all the things you like to eat and make you lunch for the week. I'll leave it with the doorman, and on the way to school you can swing by and pick it up."

"If you make me lunch, are you going to put it in a brown paper bag?"

"Do you want it in a brown paper bag?"

"Yes, I want my lunch in a brown paper bag. When kids come to school and they have their lunch in a brown paper bag, everyone knows that someone cares about them."

Two months later, Maurice had no one to go with him to his parent-teacher conference, and Laura stepped in again. In her book, she shares the conversation she had with Maurice's teacher.

"You should know that Maurice is very proud of you," the teacher said. "He speaks about you often."

"I'm very proud of him," Laura said. "He's such a special boy."

"Miss Schroff, I must say something to you. Children like Maurice are always disappointed in life. Every day someone else lets them down. I hope you realize you can't just come in and out of his life. If you are going to be there for him, you have to really be there for him. You cannot just wake up one day and abandon this boy."

"Maurice is my friend, and I would never walk out on a friend."

As Laura and Maurice became closer, Maurice began spending time with Laura's family, and it was a visit with Laura's sister, Annette, on Christmas Day that inspired him to start thinking about his future. He was amazed by what he saw—in their home in a New York suburb, Annette's family had three bathrooms all to themselves, their own washer and dryer and a room just for watching TV. Even more amazing, the whole family sat down for dinner together. At Maurice's house, no one sat down to eat, let alone together. He'd eat wherever he was when he was handed food. This was a revelation for him.

On the way home that night, Laura asked him what his favorite part of the day had been, thinking he'd say it was riding bikes or playing on the backyard swing set with Annette's kids.

"I love that room," he said.

"Which room?"

"You know, that fancy room where we had dinner."

"Oh, that's the dining room. Why did you love that room?"

"I thought the food was great, but I loved how everybody was talking and laughing and sharing. And, you know what? Someday when I grow up, I'm going to have a room just like that."

After having received only two gifts in his life—a teddy bear from the Salvation Army and a joint from his grandmother—Maurice had received many gifts that night. And the most important one was the inspiration to dream.

"At that point, I'd never looked that far down the road," Maurice says in An Invisible Thread. "I just lived from day to day. I was more worried about what I was going to eat the next day than about what I wanted to be when I grew up. I didn't know if I even would grow up, given the way I was living, but after meeting Laura, I began to broaden my view on my life. I began to think I could actually get a job of some kind. For the first time ever, I could picture myself as an adult, and maybe even see myself working."

Maurice went on to get a high school GED and graduate from college. He's now in the construction business, and he and his wife of over twenty years have seven children. He also mentors kids in community youth groups.

It all could have gone very differently if Laura had simply given him a few dollars to get something to eat. "To this day I can still feel the pain of my stomach hurting from not eating for two days. And God sent me an angel. And my angel was my mom Laura. I love her to death."

The relationship has changed Laura's life, too. "I was so lucky to meet him. I was thirty-five years old and working around the clock, and all of a sudden one day this kid came into my life and gave me this incredible different perspective and purpose in my life. Maurice opened my eyes and heart to so many things. He taught me one of the greatest lessons a person can hope to learn: He taught me to be grateful for what I have. If we could all walk in Maurice's shoes for just one day, we'd never complain about our lives again. He taught me about resilience and courage. He taught me the real meaning of lunch in a brown paper bag."

He also taught her the importance of having a big dining room table where a family eats together and shares conversation—like the one where Maurice and his family eat today.

EVERYTHING I NEED TO KNOW I LEARNED IN MY FIRST SEMESTER OF COLLEGE

Institutions have a unique opportunity because they tend to reach so many people, whether through consistent kindness or a single action that has an impact decades later. The example that Haverford College set for Howard Lutnick would reverberate eighteen years after he graduated.

When terrorists flew hijacked planes into the World Trade Center on September 11, 2001, Howard and his wife were dropping their son off for his first day of kindergarten in the Bronx. After hearing what had happened, Howard, raced to the scene to check on his employees at the financial services firm Cantor Fitzgerald, where he was president. The firm's Lower Manhattan office employed 960 people at One World Trade Center.

When he arrived, he approached people rushing out of the building, but he could find none of the 658 employees who had been in the office that day. Before long, he found himself consumed in a cloud of debris as Two World Trade Center collapsed, and he had to flee the scene.

Howard later learned that none of the employees had survived. The plane had crashed into the ninety-third floor, and Cantor Fitzgerald's offices were above the point of impact. His employees had no way to escape.

Making the situation especially heartbreaking was Cantor's policy of encouraging employees to hire friends and family—the company believes hires should be people the team would love to work with. So the survivors lost not just colleagues but friends and family. That held true for everyone from the CEO to the security guard: Howard lost his brother, security guard James Hopper lost his brother-in-law and both lost their best friends. Some siblings died together—twenty-seven sets in all. The loss could barely be comprehended.

In the wake of the tragedy, with no way to contact the employees who hadn't been in the office, the company asked media sources to announce the details of a conference call they could join. That call turned out to be pivotal.

"What I said was, 'If we are going to go back to work, it sure as heck isn't for money,'" Howard says. "'Because Lord knows I really couldn't care less about going to work and I couldn't care less about money. What I want to do is crawl into bed in a ball and just hold my family as tight as I possibly can. But if we are going to go to work, there is only one reason we are going to work, and that is we have to help the families of those we lost.' We ended up with a unanimous decision by all those who were on the phone that we were going to rebuild the company and try to have the company survive for one reason and one reason only: to try to help the families of those we lost."

After being abandoned by his own family as a college student, he knew exactly what not to do in this situation.

"My mother died when I was in eleventh grade, and Dad was killed my first week at Haverford College. My extended family pulled out. We were three children—my twenty-year-old sister, eighteen-year-old me and my fifteen-year-old brother—and they thought we'd be sticky. My uncle thought that if he reached in and he touched us and we came over for dinner, maybe we'd never leave. So they chose not to ever invite us for dinner, and I knew what it was like when people pulled out."

The administrators at Haverford, who had known Howard for only a week when he lost his father, set a different example. The president of the college called Howard immediately to tell him the college would pay for his education. The university his sister attended, on the other hand, told her that she should get a job as a waitress if she couldn't afford tuition—making Haverford's offer even more meaningful.

"Haverford College showed me what it meant to be a human being," Howard says, and he went on to demonstrate the same humanity in the wake of the 9/11 tragedy. Besides committing to being present for the families of his deceased employees and helping them financially, he personally called them and wrote thirteen hundred condolence notes by hand, to both spouses and parents. He also set up a foundation run by his sister to provide information, support and advocacy for them.

When it came to restarting the business, though—the vehicle for carrying out the financial commitment to the families—there was a low likelihood of success. The firm lacked sufficient employees and infrastructure. It also had a secure computer system, and many of the passwords had been known only by employees who had died. The off-site backups containing the password information had been in the basement of Two World Trade Center.

Howard says the company never asked for help but got it anyway. "Microsoft flew in fifty people to break into our own systems. Cisco brought in twenty 18-wheelers with every piece of hardware known to mankind and parked them as far as the eye could see [at Cantor's temporary site in New Jersey]. So if we asked for a piece of hardware and it was in Truck 12, they took a dolly and got it off."

Unfortunately, while Cantor was busy trying to rise from the ashes, competitors saw this as a great opportunity, and on Thursday, September 13, a competing bond market was opened. Civilian flights had been grounded in the U.S. for two days and the NFL and Major League Baseball had cancelled their games out of respect for those who had died, but a new bond market was opening.

Besides wanting to hold on to their customers, Cantor somehow needed to settle billions of dollars' worth of trades made on September 10 even though the records had been destroyed. So Howard's team went into overdrive. They worked around the clock in a backup data center on the site, trying to get the company's electronic trading platform for bonds online. They took naps on cots, in chairs or in their cars. And they hired more than thirty new employees that weekend.

"If they could start on Monday and they were breathing and we thought they knew what they were doing, we hired them," Howard says. It was a sprint.

Members of the London office also worked all hours, taking over jobs from their late New York colleagues and calling customers to try to keep the business going. And bankers loaned the firm $70 billion so it could settle trades.

It all paid off. On Monday, Cantor Fitzgerald was open for business with its electronic trading platform. It had no way to let clients know, though, so Howard did a media interview.

"I went on TV because I had no salespeople, had no way to tell people we were in business, and told my story and I started crying because, as it turns out, at that time when you said '658' to me I couldn't not cry. I thought, of course, I could keep it together, but whenever the number 658 was said, I started to cry. But we had to try to take care of our families."

So they were up and running, but their problems weren't over. "We were so short-staffed that when we opened for business, we had a rule that we could only do one trade per client because we didn't want to mess things up. We were a company held together with glue and bubble gum and string."

But there was a client who wouldn't take "one" for an answer.

"The woman on the other end of the phone, who works for one of the biggest money managers in America, says, 'No, no, you don't understand. Our investment committee got together this morning. We decided we're doing all of our business with you.' We said, 'No, no, no, *you* don't understand. We don't have anybody. We can't do it. We'll do a terrible job. We can't do it.' She says, 'I don't have a choice. I was ordered to do this. If you don't do it, I'll lose my job. I'm sending you by fax everything we want to do. You need to take care of it. Do the best you can. We're okay with it,' and hung up."

That day ended up being the busiest in Cantor's history. "We'd been killed with kindness," as Howard puts it. "We announced to the world that we were hungry, and everybody in the world reached out and took a little piece of bread and stuck it in our mouth."

Howard was concerned that his decimated firm would fail under the volume of trades, but the team managed to hold things together. There was even a chance that they would fulfill their mission to help the 9/11 victims' families. It had been decided that 25 percent of profits would go to the families for five years and that their health care benefits would be covered for ten years. Day One seemed to hold out hope for the mission's success.

Then Howard got a call from his Los Angeles office. All sixteen staffers were planning to attend the company's upcoming memorial service. Although, on one hand, this was a touching show of support, something told Howard that trouble was looming. Those sixteen salespeople were the best in the company's equity sector, and in a sense, they were the key to everything. If they weren't on board with the sacrifice that all the firm's employees were making for the sake of the affected families, if they weren't comfortable with the risk that the firm wouldn't recover—in other words, if they were going to turn in their resignations—it would be the beginning of the end for Cantor.

When the LA contingent got to town, they arranged to meet with Howard at his home. All he could think about was how valuable these people were to the firm.

"They were incredible. They were huge producers of revenue. They could get a job anywhere. We were a broken firm, so they could easily go across the street and make more money."

When Howard walked into the meeting room, everyone stood and gathered around him. He braced himself to hear the worst: "Howard, we love you but we're sorry—we have to leave."

But that's not what they said. What they said was "We're never leaving."

"It still gets me," Howard says. "It's unbelievable."

And yes, all sixteen are still with the firm today.

In the five years after the September 11 attacks, the Cantor Fitzgerald Relief Fund donated $180 million to the families of the employees who died at the World Trade Center. And every September 11, the firm donates 100 percent of the day's revenues to charity, which has amounted to about $159 million globally and over $12 million in 2018. The relief fund now assists people affected by natural disasters and emergencies, direct service charities and wounded members of the military. In total, it has distributed $336 million.

People often ask Howard what drove him to do so much for his employees' families.

"Haverford taught me what it was to be a human being," he says, "and September 11 opened the door for *me* to express how to be a human being."

Besides spearheading Cantor's donations, Howard has become the largest donor in Haverford College's history, having given more than $65 million. His contributions have taken the form of endowed scholarships and buildings named for his brother and two close friends who had worked for Cantor.

The way he sees it, it's nothing compared with the invaluable lesson he learned in college. "Each of us will have the opportunity to change the life of someone else. If you see it and you grab it, you can do what Haverford did for me. Haverford taught me a fundamental lesson, and there was no chance I'd miss it."

WHAT WE CAN DO

My dad taught me to be a good person. He'd lend a hand or an ear to anyone. I'm not sure he could hammer a nail, but we had an awesome collection of tools in our basement because Dad, an accountant, did a neighbor's taxes for free, for which he was given a new tool as a thank-you every year. A soldier and his family visited our house because Dad had sent him encouraging letters through a Gulf War letter-writing program. I'd be in the grocery store and people would stop me and say, "Are you Joe Aronson's son?" When I said yes, they'd say things like "Such a nice man" and "Your dad is wonderful."

We set an example simply by the way we live. Often, we're not even conscious of it—we have no idea that we're helping someone, let alone that we're sharing a moment that may change their perspective.

I've learned a tremendous amount from examples that people have set for me. Here are a few takeaway ideas that have helped me to become a better person and made me more likely to make a difference through my daily interactions:

Be aware
If you have kids, assume they're watching everything you do. They are.

Make better decisions
There are times when we can rationalize doing or saying something that we might not be proud of. A friend of mine tries to avoid that by assuming that the entire world will know every decision he makes, and another friend asks his employees to assume that all of their decisions will appear on the front page of the *Wall Street Journal*. I imagine my family will know every choice I make. Who can you imagine knowing every decision you make?

Make people believe you can levitate a table
"If you do your job well, within six months you'll be able to convince the kids that you can levitate a table." When my supervisor said this during a training session for mentors for at-risk youths, I thought it was crazy. The youths had been in trouble with the law, but they were far from stupid. It took me until the end of the session to understand what he meant. Very few people keep all or even most of their promises (even being on time). So if you become the person who keeps every commitment you make, you'll truly stand out, and if you say you're going to do something crazy—like levitate a table—people are likely to think you might actually know how to pull it off. After all, you'll be that rare person who delivers on what you say you'll do.

Tell the truth

A couple were suing my wife and me because we'd backed out of an agreement to purchase their home. It's legal to back out of a house-buying agreement, and I was furious. The husband was in real estate and knew the law, so why was he suing us? I called my friend Jon to vent and ask his opinion, and after listening, he asked a few questions. Then he told me that although I wasn't legally at fault, the situation was my fault and he explained why. I appreciate Jon's honesty. He's the guy I go to when I need advice. He tells me the truth even if I don't want to hear it. Now I try to be the person who tells friends the truth even when it would be a lot easier to just tell them what they'd like to hear.

Wave

I was waiting to cross the street one day when the driver at the intersection gave me a friendly wave to signal me to go. Usually, people signal for you to cross with a quick flick of the wrist, and I appreciate it, but it makes me feel like I should hurry and that they're letting me go because they think they have to. When this driver gave me a friendly wave, I didn't feel rushed. I felt like he was happy to give me the chance to cross and it made my morning. So I've started doing that when I stop to let pedestrians cross, and almost everyone gives me a smile and a wave back.

Be sensitive to limitations

My cousin Lianne's son Josh has a nut allergy and is usually served a dessert that pales in comparison with the other kids' dessert at birthday parties. But one day Josh had the same dessert as everyone else, and he talked about it the whole way home. And while he did all that talking, Lianne had a good cry. Dessert isn't a big deal to many of us, but when you're the kid who can never have the dessert everyone else has—or that kid's parent—it *is* a big deal. Lianne also taught me about other challenges faced by kids with food allergies:

not being able to take part in the team snack at a Little League game or being told you're the reason that your entire group isn't allowed to eat a particular food. I wish I'd thought about this earlier, but now when I'm coaching a team or throwing a party, I don't wait for parents to contact me. I ask all of them to let me know about any food allergies, and I get food everyone can enjoy together, even when parents tell me not to worry because they can bring their own child's snack. And for Halloween, in addition to candy, we've started giving out vampire teeth and other small toys. Of course, the principle is broader than food allergies. It's about being considerate of each individual's limitations, whether it's a dietary restriction or a physical disability or something else.

. . . .

We're setting an example all the time and usually we're not even thinking about it—the mom who chose the dessert that Josh could eat certainly had no idea her example would reach me, considering I was a hundred miles away at the time. But sometimes, setting an example is exactly what we have in mind. When *you* have that in mind, just look around for opportunities. They could be as close as your workplace, your neighborhood or even your home.

TAKE FIFTEEN MINUTES TO . . .

Take out a pen and paper or your phone and answer these questions: Who do you want to set an example for? What example do you want to set? What actions can you take to set that example?

LESS IS MORE THAN YOU THINK

"I opened two gifts this morning. They were my eyes."
—OFTEN ATTRIBUTED TO ZIG ZIGLAR

I WAS FINALLY on my way. I was off to meet with the CEO of a non-profit I'd been hoping to work with for years. I rarely rehearse conversations, but this time I had, and I'd also taken more care than usual with my clothes. Instead of my normal button-down shirt and jeans, I was wearing a jacket, khakis and well-polished shoes, all carefully chosen the night before. I'd also transferred all my stuff—notepad, pens, business cards, mints—from my backpack to a fancy satchel I use for situations like this. I was ready.

About thirty minutes into the drive, I noticed I was almost on "empty" and I pulled into a gas station in a rough part of North Philadelphia. This was one of those gas stations where the employees are sequestered behind a protective window along with everything that's for sale. As I got out of the car and reached for my wallet, I realized I'd forgotten it.

I checked out the surroundings. On the benches outside the entrance, a couple of guys were apparently sleeping off hangovers. I took a few deep breaths and closed my eyes. *Why am I so freakin' forgetful?*

I began tearing the car apart in search of at least a few dollars that might have been left behind. I combed the floor, scoured the trunk and dug out everything from under the seats. I even pulled out my son's car seat just in case he'd been squirreling away money there. When I was done, all I had to show for my efforts were two umbrellas, a mini ninja figure, granola bar wrappers, a handful of Angry Birds toys, a pile of crumbs I'd brushed onto the floor and fifty cents in very small change.

Sighing, I got back in the car and continued driving. Without my wallet, I also didn't have an ID, which I knew was required to get into the nonprofit's building. Oh well—at least I wouldn't have to worry about not making an impression on the CEO. When she got the call that she had a visitor who didn't have any ID, I'd make an impression before I even set foot in her office. An impression I could drive home by asking if I could bum ten bucks off her for gas. Otherwise, I might not be getting home that night.

Sometimes all you can do is laugh. Of course, it's more fun when you have someone to laugh with, so I called my wife. Mia knows all about my forgetfulness, and I figured she'd appreciate the situation.

I was right. We laughed out loud together. Then she let me in on a secret: knowing me so well, she'd stashed twenty dollars in my car for just such an occasion. I looked in the glove compartment and, sure enough, found a twenty-dollar bill hidden in there. I *would* be making it home that night.

After thanking her profusely, I drove the rest of the way to the meeting, where I experienced another stroke of luck. The CEO got out of her car at the same time as I did, so I was able to walk into the building with her and bypass the front desk, with no one any the wiser about my forgotten wallet.

That day, a little thing made the difference between appearing to be competent and appearing to be a guy who can't remember to take his wallet with him when he leaves the house. (I'm actually both, but most executives might not understand that.) And *that* made the difference between getting the opportunity to work with an exciting nonprofit and potentially getting passed over.

People talk about big birthday surprises and breathtaking holiday gifts, but give me the little things in life. To me, it's the everyday details that matter. The little things are the big things. When we realize this, we also realize that there are infinite ways to help others.

THE MENDERS

In March 2010, seventy-one-year-old Barb Lappen was newly retired and looking for a meaningful way to spend her time. When a guest speaker at her suburban Philadelphia church told stories of the work she did for Broad Street Ministry (BSM), a nonprofit dedicated to helping Philadelphia's homeless, something clicked.

"I could have served food or something like that, but it didn't engage me," Barb says. "But I do know how to sew, and maybe they had things that needed to be sewn up and mended."

When she pitched the idea to BSM staff members, they didn't know if there was a need for mending but invited her to run the idea past the guests during lunch someday.

"As lunch was served, I would go to a table and say, 'We're thinking of starting a mending project here,' and I got the most blank-looking faces. Finally someone said, 'What is mending?' I said, 'It's repairing your clothes.' And this one guy had on a jacket and he pulled it open and he said, 'You mean like this?' The whole lining of the jacket was ripped, from the wrist down to the waist. I said, 'That is exactly what we could mend for you.' Another man said, 'You mean like this?' and he pulled a button out of his pocket with some thread hanging from it. I said, 'Absolutely.'"

Just about everyone had something that needed to be mended, and thus the mending program got its start.

Barb didn't waste any time recruiting other seamstresses, almost all of them fellow grandmothers. "Every woman I asked about this said yes. I didn't have to beat the bushes. I thought that was God's hand. I had the idea, but I think God was guiding all of us."

With a crew of six menders in place, they turned their efforts to gathering the tools and materials they needed.

"People donated a lot of sewing stuff, but what we still needed were some good machines—ones that weren't forty years old," Barb says. "But we didn't have any money. So we had a pity party, and then one woman opened her pocketbook, took out a twenty-dollar bill and put it on my coffee table. She said, 'This is a start to a new machine.' Every single woman followed her lead."

When Barb's church found out about the menders, members began donating money, and the church included the group in a Christmas fundraiser. Between that and the menders' thriftiness—"We always save our coupons for JOANN!" Barb says—they soon had enough money for the sewing machines.

Over time, the group has grown to thirty menders. Five or six of them show up to work at BSM every Thursday, and a second crew shows up every week at Hub of Hope, another homeless engagement center in Philadelphia. In the morning, guests drop off items that need mending, and they usually get them back the same day.

"Homeless people have to wait for everything," Barb says. "They aren't used to being served, and so that is one of our guiding principles: to get that garment finished and back to the person in the same day. In the beginning, if they had pants that we shortened, I'd press them and put them over my arm like a valet and go out and find the person and say, 'These are your pants. They're all ready.' They'd look at me like 'What? They're ready and they're pressed and you're bringing them out on your arm?'"

For people used to being treated as if they're invisible, it's no doubt a rare pleasure to come to BSM on mending day and be offered a seat where they can relax and talk to someone who cares. The fact that the menders can fix a favorite shirt, whip an outfit into shape for a job interview or reinforce all-important pockets and backpacks is the icing on the cake.

"We mend about twelve or thirteen items every Thursday," Barb says. "And some things are more complicated than others. The backpacks come in there and you would just cry if you saw them, but we fix them. Everything they own is in their backpacks and their pockets, so pocket mending is a big deal, too."

It may sound corny, but these menders really are mending hearts as well as clothes. They learn the names of their guests, offer hugs and reassuring pats on the back and—maybe in a way that only a grandmother can—remind the guests that they're important. It's no wonder that some of the guests leave with tears in their eyes.

As one homeless man said, "Everyone appreciates them. They are amazing, great seamstresses, and they care. It's so nice to be recognized and treated like a person."

Another guest came back two years after the menders had fixed his backpack to thank them. He wanted them to know that he was employed and off the streets and that he hadn't forgotten what they'd done for him.

After ten years, the work inspires Barb as much as ever. "When we walk to the train at the end of the day to head home, we look at each other and say, 'I'm really tired, but what a good tired it is.'"

NO MORE KNOTS

While Barb's guests thrived on the fact that the menders didn't treat them as if they were invisible, there are those who *want* to be invisible. Sometimes the smallest thing we can do to help them to achieve that is the biggest favor we can do for them.

Jimmy, a kid from Flint, Michigan, wanted more than anything to blend in. Every morning before school, his mom tied his shoes in a jumble of knots in hopes that they'd stay tied all day and he wouldn't have to ask his teacher to retie them. Jimmy hated how conspicuous the big loopy knots were, but he *really* hated having his teacher retie them in front of everyone. Although tying shoes wasn't a problem for any of the other third graders, Jimmy was different from them in a significant way: he had only one hand.

His teacher, Donn Clarkson, never made him feel embarrassed about needing help, but for Jimmy, not being able to tie his own shoes was just one more reminder that he wasn't like his classmates. As if the shiny metal prosthetic "hook" hand that he tried to hide in his pocket weren't enough. It looked so foreign and threatening that it once even made one of his classmates cry.

One day when Jimmy got to school, Mr. Clarkson greeted him with a big smile. "I've got it! I figured it out!"

Jimmy had no idea what he was talking about.

"I know how you can tie your shoes," he said.

After turning on the film projector to keep the rest of the class occupied, Mr. Clarkson dragged two chairs into the hallway, where he invited Jimmy to sit and taught him how to tie his shoes with just his left hand.

Whether it had taken Mr. Clarkson twenty minutes or all night to figure out, it had a profound effect on Jim Abbott's life. "I know it doesn't sound like a big deal," Jim says decades later, "but he had two hands. And I think of him at night . . . with a clenched fist and working with those laces and pulling them tight, and then coming that day and pulling me out of class and saying, 'We can do this.'"

Jim says Donn Clarkson's gift was a turning point. It instilled a belief in him that he'd always be able to find a solution for whatever problems he faced. This attitude that there wasn't anything he couldn't do would go on to fuel a stellar career. Jim won an Olympic gold medal as part of the American baseball team, played Major League Baseball, pitched a no-hitter, wrote a best-selling memoir and touched the lives of thousands of people through his inspirational talks and volunteerism.

When Jim had signed his first contract with the California Angels, he became an instant point of curiosity and inspiration for children who looked different from their friends. Suddenly, children who were born with visible congenital anomalies or had suffered permanent injuries had a hero and a role model.

The letters from children and their parents started arriving during spring training. "First, there were a couple letters at a time," Jim says in his inspiring autobiography, *Imperfect: An Improbable Life,* "and Tim Mead (then director of media relations for the team) would bring them by my locker and we'd write back something supportive and personal."

By the time the season started, a couple of letters a week had turned into dozens, and soon there would be hundreds. "I read every letter," Jim writes, "and Tim and I answered every one because I knew these kids and I knew how far a little boy or girl could run with fifty words of reassurance."

Before long, children with disabilities were showing up at every game. Jim was caught off guard.

"I didn't expect the stories they told or the distance they traveled to tell them or the desperation revealed in them. They were shy and beautiful, and they were loud and funny, and they were, like me, somehow imperfectly built. And, like me, they had parents nearby, parents who willed themselves to believe that this accident of circumstance or nature was not a life sentence, and that the spirits inside these tiny bodies were greater than the sums of their hands and feet."[2]

Jim played ten seasons, and whether he was playing well or not, he always took the time to talk to the kids and sometimes even show them how to tie their shoes with one hand. And for every kid he met, there were many others who saw him on TV.

One of the kids Jim inspired, Nick Newell, had been born without a left hand. He was six years old when he saw Jim on TV, and at that point Jim was the only other person Nick had seen who had only one hand. He got the chance to meet Jim when his grandparents took him to a Yankees meet-and-greet and Jim took the time to visit with them—and, in the process, provide Nick with some inspiration. If Jim could play for Nick's favorite baseball team, Nick could pursue *his* dreams.

When Nick was older, he joined the school wrestling team. He lost his first seventeen matches, getting pinned every time, but he kept pushing. "I wasn't good at it, and the competitor in me was not okay with that," he says. "I had to keep working and become good at it. Over the summer, while other kids were playing around, I was training."

The next year he had a winning record, and in his senior year he broke school and state records and made All-State. In college, he captained his team and also had the chance to train in mixed martial arts (MMA). He lost his first MMA fight, but he won the next thirteen.

Despite his success, though, Nick wasn't allowed to compete in the Ultimate Fighting Championship (UFC), the best-known and highest-paying league. "It's hard to fight here with *two* arms," UFC President Dana White said. "Fighting with one arm is just craziness to me." But Nick didn't let that stop him. Instead, he fought his way to a world championship in Xtreme Fighting Championships. Six years later, White would change his mind and give Nick a chance to earn a contract with UFC—if he could win a fight against undefeated fighter Alex Munoz. Unfortunately, Nick lost in a close match, but he's still hoping to land a UFC contract.

"I just think of myself as a regular guy who wants to be the best he can be," Nick says. "The amount of hands I have really makes no difference. I am a fighter who happens to have one hand, not a one-handed fighter. But it does make a difference to other people. There are people that get discouraged and look at me and say, 'Hey, if this guy can do it, I can do it.'"

That's how Nick had regarded Jim. "I looked at him when I was a kid and it helped me. I had never seen anyone else that only had one hand. Then all of a sudden I meet Jim, and he has one hand. I thought he was awesome, and he showed me that I could be what I wanted to be."

And now Nick finds *himself* a role model. "I didn't expect it, but all these people started coming out, and I always go out of my way to meet people who want to meet me. Jim met *me*. He showed me how to behave if you become a success. What makes me any better than anyone? I was just a kid who wanted to meet someone, and I met him and it changed me. Because of the impact he had on me, I'd like to do that for someone else."

In addition to being a favorite in the World Series of Fighting, Nick meets kids with upper limb loss and their families at events run by the nonprofit Helping Hands and speaks at seminars across the United States. Like his role model, he continues to work with and inspire children, showing them by example that even the biggest dreams can be achieved.

And sometimes he even passes along Donn Clarkson's lesson and teaches them how to tie their shoes with one hand.

ANGEL FROM ANOTHER WORLD

When Jim talks about Don's lesson, he begins, "I know it doesn't sound like a big deal," but no one knows better than he does how big a deal his teacher's gesture was. If something doesn't sound like a big deal, think again. Literally. Take a moment to consider that it might be a big deal after all—and to remember that we need to get past drop-in-the-bucket thinking if we're going to see all the opportunities out there for what they are.

Those opportunities can be found at your school, your church or anywhere else in your community. They're as close as your husband's glove compartment (thanks, Mia) and as far away as another continent. Hilde Back found opportunity both in her backyard in Sweden and thousands of miles away in Africa, where a monthly act of kindness she performed transformed Chris Mburu's life—and ultimately the lives of hundreds of others.

As a child in Kenya, surrounded by families earning barely enough to feed themselves, Chris was on a well-worn path. In his village, which lacked paved roads, electricity, running water and medical facilities, families couldn't afford the fees required for secondary school. Instead of finishing school, most kids would wind up working in the fields, following in their parents' footsteps and sometimes not even making enough money to survive.

"Not much hope for a future," Chris says.

Meanwhile, more than four thousand miles and a world away in Sweden, Hilde Back knew firsthand what it was like to grow up without hope. As a Jewish teenager in Germany in the 1940s, she was trapped amid the horrors of the Holocaust—until a stranger gave her family money so that she and her parents could cross the Baltic Sea and join her brothers, who were already living in Sweden.

Because she was only seventeen, Hilde was admitted into the country while her parents were sent back to Germany, where they would die in separate concentration camps. In their absence, a family friend arranged for Hilde to become a nanny for a Swedish couple with a young child.

As an adult, Hilde became a preschool teacher and went on to help children and support her community. She gave what she could to charitable organizations such as Save the Children, and in the early 1970s when she learned of a Swedish nonprofit to support gifted and impoverished Kenyan children by paying their school fees, she signed on.

"I think it's very important to care about people in other countries and other cultures," Hilde said in an interview with *The Jewish Chronicle.* "I was helped once when I came to Sweden. And it affects you very much . . . . I think there's so much need in the world that we need to help. It just felt normal to donate some money to a child."

So every four months, she sent a $15 gift to support a boy more than four thousand miles away. "It wasn't much money," she says in *A Small Act,* a documentary about the results of her act of kindness. "What you send is just a drop in the ocean, and sometimes you wonder whether it helps." But her gift was enough to alter the path Chris was on. In fact, it was enough to change *everything* for the star student. By making it possible for Chris to attend high school, Hilde also made it possible for him to attend the University of Nairobi, which is free, and graduate from Harvard Law School on a Fulbright scholarship.

To those who knew her in Sweden, Hilde was a quiet school-teacher. To Chris, she was "an angel who walked into my life and fixed it." He said the $15 she sent every school term is what made him who he is. "Some stranger walked into my life and changed it," he told Movies that Matter. "Hilde gave me hope. I kept coming back to the village and seeing these people that I went to school with who had not been able to continue with their studies, and I saw where they were in their lives. For them, the angel had not appeared." Now, Chris is doing something about that. At age fifty-three, he's an international human rights lawyer serving with the United Nations as a senior human rights adviser. He's also the founder of a nonprofit that assists with education funding for Kenyan children living in poverty. In his spare time, he advocates for governments around the world to provide free education as a basic human right, and he raised awareness through events in more than a dozen countries last year. "I want to see a world in which children have equal opportunity and are not robbed of their future by poverty, like so many of my friends in the village were," Chris said.

In *A Small Act*, he talks about having to tackle a big problem with the same kind of approach that Hilde did. "We would like to be able to support the education of every student, but we need to start small. You have to say, 'I know that I cannot provide support, relief and help to all the suffering that is around here, but I want to do one thing. I want to take one action that will work towards relieving that situation.'"

At the time of the fund's founding in 2001, Chris hadn't met his benefactor, but he knew her name and called his nonprofit the Hilde Back Education Fund in her honor. He didn't know if she was even alive, but he petitioned the Swedish embassy to find her, and after it shared her contact information with him, he reached out to her. They've since become close friends. In fact, Chris considers their relationship to be like that of a mother and son, and he makes a point of taking the long trip from home to visit her in Sweden at least once a year. One year he also accompanied her on a trip to his Kenyan village, where she was made an honorary tribal elder. She dressed in traditional Kikuyu clothes, and the village turned out for a ceremony in tribute to her. Hilde says she discovered a home she'd never known.

For Chris, meeting Hilde was an eye-opening experience. "I was not brought up in an environment where people just helped other people with whom they were not related," he says in the documentary. "I thought that Hilde was a wealthy person who was just sort of shedding off some of her wealth by supporting needy kids. And then I discover later on that she was just an ordinary Swede who probably could have found better uses for that money but she decided to use it to support a kid."

Today, Chris's nonprofit is providing opportunities for families and their future children to escape poverty just as Hilde did for him. As of 2019, the Hilde Back Education Fund has made it possible for more than eight hundred Kenyan children to be educated.

Chris says many of the students and families give back. "I get notes like 'I would like you to know that I'm so happy you helped my son, and now that we have some money, I'm sending you a little' and 'You helped me—now I will help three kids in your program.'" A group of alumni of the program have even started a club to help carry forward the organization's mission. And just like Hilde's kindness gave birth to the Hilde Back Education Fund, Chris's nonprofit is starting to give birth to additional organizations. One graduate is starting a similar nonprofit in Mombasa, the second-largest city in Kenya, and Kathleen Hubbard-Ismail, an American inspired by Chris's story, started the Ghana Scholarship Fund, which provides Ghanaian children in rural areas with educational opportunities.

"He's such an example of how someone's life can be transformed through education," Kathleen says. "And I looked at Hilde and thought, 'Heck, she's not some rich woman. She's just a person with a heart who wanted to try to make a difference.' I had taken a service trip to Ghana and had seen the education problem there and decided I, too, could do something. I told myself to just do it and don't be afraid. Never in a million years did I think I'd start a nonprofit company, let alone in Africa." With limited resources, Kathleen has built a nonprofit that has provided 190 scholarships as well as computer labs to allow hundreds of kids in rural villages to use learning software to prepare for high school.

Chris couldn't be happier that that's the kind of influence he's had. "Real philanthropists, in my view, do not have to wait to make millions to begin donating to a just cause," he says. "It's not about the size of the pocket. They can start at any time with small gestures towards the rest of humanity."

EYESIGHT TO THE POOR

Sharing Hilde's passion for giving back, my grandmother often donated modest amounts of money to charity. Nanny told us that it all mattered, and I loved that she was so thoughtful about choosing the best places for her $25 donations.

But donations weren't all she provided. She also regularly shared her wisdom with family members. I'll never forget the warm Tuesday night when I was the beneficiary of some of Nanny's well-meaning health advice. As I often did that summer, I was participating in the Philadelphia Inline Skate Club's weekly Rollerblade skate through the city, and we were about halfway through and on a drink break. I knew I had about ten minutes, and as I stood outside a convenience store drinking a Gatorade, I took advantage of that window to check in with Nanny, who was eighty-five at the time.

"Brad, I'm so happy you called," she said. "I have some important information to share." She paused. "I think your underwear is too tight. That's why you're having trouble having babies."

What?!

Fortunately, I wasn't drinking my Gatorade at that moment or I would have sprayed it all over the passersby. I didn't know what to say. Finally, the best I could come up with was, "Thanks, I'll wear looser underwear."

Nanny was always helpful that way. She'd never gone to medical school or held a health-related job, but whenever it came to matters of health, she was eager to assist family members and strangers alike. Once, she even cured a case of blindness thousands of miles away in Ethiopia.

Congenital cataracts had left an eight-year-old girl named Nunu blind since she was a toddler. In many developing countries, communities don't understand disabilities, so kids like Nunu are often stigmatized and miss out on play and school. To make matters worse, safety measures are often lacking, making it dangerous to walk in areas with cliffs and open fires. It's also a burden on family members who have to sacrifice work and school time to be with the child who is disabled.

"I had to depend on my family to walk and move around," Nunu says.[3] "In most cases, I preferred staying at home the whole day. I had no chance to go out and play with friends. They would not let me play with them even if I wanted to, because of my blindness. Everyone laughed at me. I was not given a chance to go to school, because I am blind. No one bothered to help me. I used to cry every time I heard children talking about school, and I was always worried about what will happen to me in the future."

Without the infrastructure in place to accommodate special needs, many blind children in countries like Ethiopia grow up in a world of isolation. And as adults, the blind can't contribute to supporting a family and aren't considered good prospects for marriage. All in all, it's a bleak picture.

Fortunately for Nunu, her family didn't give up hope. In response to an outreach campaign by the nonprofit Himalayan Cataract Project (HCP), she and her father traveled to the city of Harar in December

2016, where she and more than twelve hundred other people were offered hope in the form of free cataract surgery. The procedure takes about ten minutes, meaning a single doctor can perform dozens of surgeries a day. Put another way, a single doctor can transform dozens of lives a day.

When Nunu's surgery was over, she spoke like someone who'd just stepped across the threshold into a new world.

"I couldn't figure out what I was feeling at first. At the beginning, I was shocked because I never thought I would see again. Now I am the happiest girl in the entire world and I can't wait to go back home and show all my friends that I can see just like they do. I know they would let me play with them this time. I also want to go to school. I am so excited."

And where does Nanny fit into all this? With money she left me after she died, I donated $200 to HCP. Based on my calculations, HCP has brought the surgery's total cost per patient to a maximum of $195 to operate on both eyes—compared with the more than $3,000 charged per eye for the procedure in the United States. And that's $195 if HCP's entire budget is spent on surgeries, but it isn't. HCP also provides eye exams and basic eye care for nearly 1.7 million people and trains physicians who will provide life-changing eye surgeries, so the actual figure for curing a case of blindness is something *less* than $195.[4]

Chances are, Nanny's money didn't go to Nunu herself, but it was enough to cure someone *like* Nunu of blindness. For less than $100 per eye, HCP has restored vision to hundreds of thousands of people across Asia and Sub-Saharan Africa. Besides providing volunteer doctors and setting up temporary clinics in remote areas, the program trains local physicians and health care providers in the cataract-removal procedure, creating a structure that can be sustained long after HCP is gone.

Currently, eighteen million people are still waiting for HCP's life-changing procedure. That's eighteen million opportunities for caring people like Nanny to donate less than $200 and change a life. Or if we don't have $200, we can round up twenty friends and each donate $10 toward curing blindness. It's the opportunity of a lifetime in more ways than one.

A JAR OF HOPE

Sue Ingalsbe can also attest to the power of small gestures. All within three years, she lost her parents, her marriage and her house and was diagnosed with breast cancer. Everything was falling apart at once, and as much as she tried to believe things would get better, she eventually lost hope. She no longer believed her life would improve, let alone ever be normal again. She felt alone and invisible.

"I was working six days a week to put food on the table, to pay my medical insurance to cover my ongoing cancer expenses and to cover other bills," Sue says. "I'm a social worker and worked as an elder-care case manager and consultant during the week and as a waitress every Saturday and occasionally for special events on Sunday. I was exhausted."

Despite working all those hours, she was barely scraping by. When the holiday season arrived, it made things even worse. Everywhere, there were reminders that other people were leading happy lives, reminders that other families would be spending Christmas together.

A few days after hitting what she describes as an all-time low, she received a package in the mail. It was a heavy box wrapped in brown packing paper, and there was no return address. She set it on the floor of the spare bedroom of the friend's house where she was staying and cut through the packing tape with scissors. When she lifted the flaps of the box, there was a sheet of packing paper covering the contents. Underneath, she found a plastic peanut butter jar decorated with wrapping paper. It was packed with pennies, nickels, dimes, quarters and crinkled paper money.

She gasped. *Who would do this for me?*

Accompanying the jar was a simple note: "Use this for yourself."

As she hugged the jar, she noticed that it still smelled a little like peanut butter, and the tears began. She *wasn't* invisible. Somebody had seen her struggling and cared about her enough to help.

The jar turned out to contain $157.52, but Sue also found something far more valuable inside.

"It gave me hope. I felt loved and cared about, and that meant so much to me in such a desperate time. I didn't know who it was from, but I didn't feel alone anymore."

The gesture also reassured her of something she'd started to lose sight of: "It renewed my faith in mankind."

Sue used the money for food and bills, but she also kept some in the jar. The day after Christmas, she added more change to it, and over the course of the following year she continued to add to it until it contained $127. At that point, she anonymously passed the jar on to someone who she knew didn't have money to buy Christmas gifts for his children. She took great joy in seeing that those children got a visit from Santa that year anyway.

And if the anonymous party who had given the jar to Sue the previous year has seen the impact of *that* gesture, they've seen her transformation from a woman who had given up on life to a woman determined to share her good fortune. Sue has made the filling of the Christmas jar an annual tradition, and she encloses a simple note of her own to encourage the recipient to continue the cycle of "paying it forward."

"Every day that I look at the jar I'm filling with money, I remember the difference it made in my life. That's the true meaning of Christmas. I'm reminded of Christmas every day of the year, and I hope to pass that joy on to others."

As Sue later learned, the "Christmas jar" is an idea sparked by the book *Christmas Jars*, by Jason Wright. Since its publication in 2005, the book has inspired people across the world to adopt the tradition, and there are now hundreds of stories online about people who have received Christmas jars and begun giving away jars of their own.

"It's about keeping hope alive and the goodness of people," Sue says. "The money was a huge help to me, but it wasn't what mattered the most. It made such a difference not to feel so desperate and alone anymore. Someone understood what I was going through and wanted to help. That simple little blessing gave me hope that things were going to be okay."

WHAT WE CAN DO

My grandfather had lunch with his friends at Subway every week—until the sandwich prices went up. In the face of this outrage, they switched to Wendy's, and the new arrangement couldn't have made Popop happier. He'd regularly tell us why Wendy's was the best deal around: "You can get an entire lunch for ninety-nine cents. I buy the ninety-nine-cent chili and get a cup of water, which is free, to go with it." His friends would do the same, and then they'd spend hours talking at a table. Sometimes the staff would even give them free Frosty drinks (which made me a lifelong Wendy's fan).

My grandfather taught me so much and was such a kind person that, every year on his birthday, we talk about him and try to do especially kind things for other people. After dinner on one of those birthdays, Mia announced that it was dessert time and pulled Frosties out of the freezer. We'd been so busy that day that we hadn't even talked about Popop, but she made time to sneak out and pick up Frosties. It was an awesome gesture, and it meant a lot to me.

Whether through your time and effort like Mia or through monetary donations like Nanny, here are some small acts of kindness that will be a big deal to the people in your life:

Learn to listen better

Everyone wants to be heard, but it's rare that we're fully heard. Here's a way to truly listen: Wait three to five seconds to see if someone is finished speaking before you respond. Waiting those few seconds is hard, but it will completely change how you listen and eliminate unintentional interruptions. It's a gift you can give to anyone, and it literally costs only seconds.

Acknowledge the people in your life

Write ten to fifty things you love about someone. Put each reason on a separate piece of paper and put them in an envelope or a small jar. Tell the person to take one from the jar anytime they could use a boost.

Share the positive

Tim, a friend who used to be a teacher, told me that when his students were doing really well he'd call their parents. He taught at an alternative school where parents usually received calls from the school when their children were in trouble, but he made sure he also called with good news—pretty great for both the kids and their parents. Look for the positive every day and share it with the people you care about. What can you share this week?

Invest

This is one you can do for people you don't even know. In the spirit of Nanny, who was so conscious of value that she sent me restaurant coupons for my entire adult life, I've chosen eleven nonprofits for the *HumanKind* Hall of Fame where donations have an outsize impact. It's amazing what we can do individually or with a group of friends thanks to organizations like those in the Hall of Fame—$500 can provide treatment that allows a child to walk, $200 will cure blindness and $20 will provide a year's participation in a childhood literacy program. Check them out on page 206.

....

The little things are often the most meaningful, and the key to finding these opportunities is remembering to look for them.

....

Who do you want to do something for just because they're awesome? Start with your friends and family. After you choose the people, consider what matters to them—not what you'd like if you were them but what actually matters to *them*. Think only about this for at least ten minutes and you'll come up with multiple small, meaningful ideas. What are your ideas? Can you perform one of them now? If not, set a date when you will.

....

CHAPTER

THE BEST MEDICINE

"Friendship isn't a big thing. It's a million little things."
—UNKNOWN

DURING MIA'S TREATMENT, one of my most difficult tasks was simply to pretend everything was normal. When the social workers told me that one of the best things I could do for Jack was to maintain routine—that if he saw me proceeding as usual, he'd take his cues from me—the concept made perfect sense. But carrying it out was easier said than done.

After being at the hospital all day, I'd put on my happy face and pick Jack up from school like Mia had always done. At home, we'd spend a couple of hours playing games before having dinner, and then we'd play games again until Jack went to bed. By the end of it all, I'd be exhausted, often falling asleep reading him a story. Then I'd drag myself out of his room to make his lunch for the next day before collapsing into my own bed.

Although I was using all my might to hold the routine together, things fell between the cracks. For example, I missed the email about the school Valentine's Day party and bought a box of candy hearts for each kid in the class when, as it turned out, we'd been specifically told not to send any food. I also failed to realize that Jack's pants didn't fit anymore until a friend pointed out the six-inch gap between his ankles and his pant cuffs. Nor did I realize there would be such a commotion about the bag of giant water guns I brought to school pickup—fully loaded—for an after-school gunfight. It's common sense that things that look like guns wouldn't be allowed at school, but somehow it never occurred to me.

After Mia got out of the hospital, she couldn't do as much around the house as she had before, and it was still very difficult for us to cover all the bases, so when my cousin Betsy told me about a camp program Jack could enroll in over the upcoming holiday break, we jumped at the opportunity. Mia still needed to go back to the hospital four times a week for chemotherapy, and this way I could take her while Jack was at camp.

But then something else fell between the cracks: By the time I got around to trying to register Jack, the camp was full. When I asked about the possibility of admitting one more camper, I was told that, by law, the camp couldn't exceed the maximum child-to-counselor ratio.

I was crushed. This meant Jack would be home every day for the two-week break and would have to come to some chemo appointments—appointments that would probably be disturbing for a five-year-old. He'd see lots of sick people hooked up to machines and generally fighting for their lives, and worse, he'd suddenly see how vulnerable his mom was. She'd done an amazing job of being strong in front of him, but now the reality of it could pull the rug out from under him, leaving him terrified of what any given day might bring. All because I'd lost track of a logistical detail.

What to do? These were the early days of Mia's treatment, and I was too frantic about her situation to think smartly about logistics, so even though my parents and in-laws had made it clear that we couldn't possibly ask too much of them, I just put my head down and shifted into get-it-done mode. But before I could come up with a solution, Betsy texted me.

"Is Jack excited for camp?"

Glumly, I responded: "Camp was filled up by the time I registered."

And then she wrote something unexpected: "There's no way Jack's not going to camp."

I had no idea what she was thinking, but three hours later she called and I found out. "Jack is going to camp," she said. "I'm donating the days I booked for Charlotte, and my friends are donating days they booked for their kids."

For some of these moms—these moms I didn't even know—it no doubt meant using vacation days to stay home from work to care for their kids. It was the definition of "the kindness of strangers," and I was touched to the core.

And the best part was that when Betsy later called to tell the camp what she was doing and about Mia's situation, the staff found a way to make room so no one had to give up days. When all was said and done, I was able to slip my happy face back on with no effort at all.

During Mia's two and a half years of chemotherapy, she was administered more medications than I can count, but the kind of "medicine" provided by Betsy and her friends was as potent as any of them. While doctors gave Mia the power to endure physically, loved ones and strangers gave us the power to endure emotionally. It's all critical to the recovery mind-set, so it's all lifesaving medicine.

It's surprisingly easy to help save a life. It can be as simple as picking up a few extra coffees on your next Starbucks run and raising some chemo patients' spirits. Then again, it can be as difficult as pouring your heart and soul into a project designed to spare countless lives from fatal diseases over generations. We all have different gifts to give—what's important is rising to the occasion, whatever circumstances we find ourselves in.

MATCHMAKER, MATCHMAKER, MAKE ME A MATCH

About a year out of college, twenty-two-year-old Jay Feinberg was working in finance and had recently been accepted to law school. In short, he felt like many new college grads: invincible and ready to take on the world.

But then he got sick. Suffering from abdominal pain and body aches, he thought he had a severe case of the flu. When he went to the hospital for testing, though, he was diagnosed with something else: leukemia.

"It was overwhelming," Jay says twenty-eight years later. "I heard that hematologist's words, but I was sort of in a dreamlike state trying to absorb it all."

The part of the conversation he remembers is when the physician said a bone marrow transplant could save his life. The doctor explained the transplant process and told him he needed to find someone with matching marrow. The place to start would be with his two brothers because there's a one-in-four chance that a sibling will be a match.

After Jay was discharged and told his brothers about the situation, they had their marrow tested, but neither was a match. Next, the Feinbergs had every family member they knew tested and began an extensive search to find relatives they *didn't* know. Working with the Jewish Genealogical Society and other experts in genealogy, they found multiple branches of the family they hadn't known about, including a contingent in Australia they thought had been wiped out in the Holocaust. All told, more than two hundred family members were tested, but none was a match.

The next step was to try to find an unrelated donor—someone willing to give of themselves to save the life of a stranger they might never have the opportunity to meet. There were national and international registries to check for matches, and Jay was hopeful.

"But that's when the second blow came," he says. "The doctor told me that there was no match in the registry—either the national registry or the international registries. He went on to add that it was going to be very difficult for me to find a match because I was Jewish."

His parents and siblings were crowded into the tiny exam room at the time, and they all exchanged baffled looks. Transplant discrimination?

"Then he explained that your tissue type is inherited like the color of your eyes or your hair, and your best chance of finding a match would be finding someone who shares a similar ethnic background. And the registry wasn't really ethnically or racially diverse." And the lack of diversity extended to Jews of Eastern European descent.

The doctor was realistic with them. He said there wasn't much that could be done in the long term without a donor. There was medicine that could keep Jay alive, but eventually the leukemia would kill him. The doctor said a donor might or might not pop up and suggested Jay go home and think about the things he'd always wanted to do in life. In other words: start making the bucket list.

"He knew a lot about medicine, he knew a lot about transplants, he knew a lot about donor searches," Jay says, "but there was one thing he didn't know: a phenomenon we refer to as the Jewish mother effect. My mother's response to the doctor was that we were going to run drives in the Jewish community and we were going to try to increase the representation of the Jewish people (in the registries) so that I'd have the opportunity to find a match and so would countless others."

And so Arlene and Jack Feinberg launched an international search to find their son a match, setting up headquarters in the living room and dining room of their New Jersey home. Jack even retired a few years earlier than planned to devote all his time to the search. (Arlene was already retired.) On any given day, six to twelve volunteers also regularly worked out of every corner of the Feinbergs' home, and Jay joined them when he wasn't in treatment. These were the days before social media, so it was mostly phone calls and faxes to find organizations willing to host and promote bone marrow registry drives.

Their local Jewish Federation also pitched in, helping to run the first drive at a nearby synagogue, and Jay's team seized the moment. They called newspapers to do publicity and asked the synagogue to send fliers home with congregants. Supporters in the community enlarged copies of the flier and hung them in storefronts and on telephone poles.

"When we got to the drive that day, the turnout was incredible—volunteers coming out to save the life of someone that they didn't necessarily know," Jay says. "And at the time, you couldn't check to see if someone was a match with a simple saliva test, so we were drawing blood, yet the line went out the door down the sidewalk into the street, and the local police were there for crowd control. It was an unbelievable feeling that so many people were willing to do that."

Because bone marrow registration drives were relatively new and the grassroots nature of this one was so inspiring, the drive captured the media's attention. The Feinbergs received calls from media outlets all over the world, and before they knew it, the publicity had created an international interest in running drives to find Jay a match. On top of that, donations came pouring in to cover the cost of processing the tests. "We got sacks and sacks and sacks of letters with checks in them and sometimes big plastic containers from the post office," Jay says.

A local builder, Dave Cali, even called to see if they were interested in having some office space. When the Feinbergs checked out the space, they found two thousand square feet that was home to furniture, copiers, printers and a phone system. There was one catch, though.

"I have to tell you that, unfortunately, we can't donate it," Dave said. "But we have a lease here, and we think the rent will be agreeable."

Oh boy, Jay thought as he and his parents traded skeptical looks.

He looked at the lease. The rent was $1 a year.

"We signed that lease very, very quickly," he says.

While chemotherapy kept Jay alive for the next four years, his parents and dozens of volunteers—which included a stay-at-home mom who came in a few times a week with her baby—worked out of the office recruiting potential donors for the worldwide registry and coordinating drives across the United States and in Canada, Australia, South Africa, Israel, England and even Tokyo. They also sent test kits to people who couldn't make it to an event and then processed the kits, and they found lifesaving matches for more than a hundred people.

But not one of the donors they found was a match for Jay, and his health was rapidly deteriorating. Finally, his physicians decided to proceed with the transplant with a less-than-perfect match because he'd soon be too sick to survive the procedure.

Around that same time, he got a call from a college student in Chicago named Benjy Merzel, whose friend was alive only because Jay's family had found him a bone marrow match.

"He told me he was going to close that circle and find my match," Jay says. "He was determined."

Benjy said he and some friends and neighbors were traveling to the Wisconsin Institute for Torah Study in Milwaukee in a couple of days to sponsor a drive. Jay expressed his appreciation and emphasized that although the drive might not benefit him, it could help others in need.

About 130 people turned out for the drive, and the last person to be tested was Becky Faibisoff, one of the neighbors who'd come with Benjy. She'd been putting it off because she was afraid of needles.

"At the very end of the drive as they were packing away the supplies, she said, 'I want to do this. Do it fast,'" Jay says. "Two weeks later, we learned that Becky was my match."

And his hero. "She shows the power of an individual and that it takes only one person to make a difference in this world."

Thanks to Becky, he'd gotten his life back, and now he could finally get started on his law degree, right? "After my transplant, I got a call from the law school saying, 'So you've had your transplant, you're healthy again. We've got your seat—when are you coming?' And it was a decision that was relatively easy for me and probably would have been for many people in my circumstances. We had built such a tremendous force here thanks to the generosity and compassion of countless strangers that we couldn't stop there."

Jay took a pass on law school and the Feinbergs kept Gift of Life going.

The organization has come a long way from the days when it was manned from the Feinbergs' dining room table. At that time, there was less than a 5 percent chance that a Jewish person would find a bone marrow match. Today, more than 70 percent of Jewish patients find a match, and more than three thousand five hundred people have found potentially lifesaving matches through Gift of Life. The organization has also helped other minorities recruit marrow donors to improve the potential for them to find matches.

The Feinbergs haven't just saved lives. They've created a *mechanism* for saving lives—one with the potential to be used for generations to come. And it's become Jay's life's work. He and his team of sixty-five employees run more than two thousand drives a year to add donors to the registry, and there's more expansion in store. Their new headquarters will include a stem cell collection center, and they're developing plans for a facility to store the cells so they can reach patients faster and more efficiently.

In short, they want to be ready for anything. "Life throws some curves," Jay says. "That's the reason I go to work every day."

DAN THE COFFEE MAN

Jay made a beautiful sacrifice for others, but you don't have to walk away from a potential law career to make a difference. You can just fit it into your errands. That's how Dan Dewey did it thirteen years ago while accompanying his father during a chemotherapy session.

"I'm going for coffee," he announced as he stood and looked around at the other patients sitting in their blue infusion chairs in the treatment room of the Michigan Cancer Institute (MCI), in Pontiac. "I have my dad's wallet. Anyone want anything?"

He got only a few takers—apparently, the others didn't feel as free to spend his dad's money as he did.

When he came back from Starbucks, he handed out the coffees he'd picked up, and as it turned out, that was the start of something much bigger. In the thirteen years since, Dan has handed out more than twenty-five thousand cups of Starbucks—and gotten at least as many smiles—at MCI and other facilities.

"I'm retired, and this is what I want to do," he says. "My gift is being silly. The stuff that used to get me in trouble as a kid, the smart remarks and trying to be funny—it really works in these places. I'll do it as long as they don't lock me out of the buildings."

When it all started, Dan's father was receiving chemotherapy for his second cancer diagnosis. It had been five years since his first treatment, and Dan recognized the same faces at the cancer center: the doctors, nurses, physicians' assistants and office staff. "I wanted to show them proper respect as well as offering to treat each patient, their families and friends to something."

During the two months of his dad's weekly chemotherapy, Dan made coffee runs every week. Eventually, he was bringing back twenty drinks per trip. And when the chemotherapy was over, he knew he couldn't stop. In fact, he didn't just continue the runs—over the years, he's expanded to seventy-five coffees a week in four runs to another cancer center and a nonprofit dedicated to helping abused and neglected children, in addition to MCI.

For years, none of Dan's friends knew about his coffee runs. Other than the recipients, only the baristas at Starbucks were wise to him, having noticed that he would show up at the same time on the same days every week. But he knew his cover was blown when he arrived one day at the usual time and the staff told him he couldn't order yet because a local television crew hadn't shown up yet—one of the baristas had called the station to tell them about Dan.

When the news crew arrived, they followed him on his run, and the resulting TV spot brought a windfall Dan's way. When he arrived at Starbucks for his regular pickup the next week, a crowd of people was waiting for him.

"All these people were handing me money. The first guy was this big construction guy who gave me a hundred dollars and said, 'Dan, spend it any way you want.' There were parents with kids, senior citizens, people who were on their way to work and all sorts of folks eager to support me."

The timing couldn't have been more perfect. That same week, Dan had run out of money—he didn't know how he could keep up the deliveries. But thanks to the media coverage that began with the local news spot, donations have been rolling in ever since and his deliveries have continued uninterrupted.

"It mystifies me," he says. "I just get up and go and it happens. Just yesterday, two women and a guy in line handed me money at the register."

Donations have come from all corners. Starbucks itself donated $10,000 worth of drinks after Dan appeared on *The Queen Latifah Show*, and a Starbucks barista at one of Dan's regular stops set up a "Dan's Coffee Run" Facebook page and an accompanying donation process. The page tells the story:

> *After three years of people asking about why this man buys so many drinks, me telling them the story and them asking how they can donate, I came up with an idea. I would get a custom Starbucks card with "Dan's Coffee Run" on it for anyone who would like to donate money that will go directly to purchasing drinks for the patients of MCI. If you are interested in donating, please see one of the baristas at the counter and they can tell you how to do it. Thanks, Valerie*

The Facebook page and now a variety of related sites raising money for Dan are also forums for talking about the impact of those coffees. A post by Liz Scroczynski seems to sum up the sentiments of so many: "I received coffee a few times from Dan when I was at the

Rose Center. Sometimes that drink was the only thing that got me through the day!"

Dan has also posted stories about the people he meets as he carries out his mission. There's one that beautifully captures the ripple effect that his coffee runs have had. In it, a young girl named Natalie approached him at a Starbucks along with her mother and younger brother. She was holding out a gift-wrapped package, and her mother explained that Natalie wanted Dan to have it.

"I stared at the package and was a bit lost," Dan says. "Although I do spend a lot of time aimlessly talking, I was somewhat speechless."

It seemed that Natalie had heard about Dan's coffee runs and, for her recent birthday party, asked that instead of gifts, all her friends bring Starbucks gift cards that she could pass on to him. Her friends were eager to support the cause, and on this day she presented Dan with the results of their generosity.

When he opened the package, he found $250 worth of gift cards inside.

"Even now I'm a bit speechless at how unselfish this was," he says.

Coming from the man who got the ball rolling during that historic coffee run in 2006, that's saying something.

WASH YOUR FACE, BRUSH YOUR TEETH, BE NICE

Of course, if you're retired like Dan, you have the option of doing like he did and building a schedule *around* kind acts. If you're not retired, you can work kind acts *into* your schedule.

During Mia's treatment, our neighbor Vicki would call when she was headed to the grocery store and ask if there was anything she could pick up for us. She made it easy to say yes. Her choice of words made it absolutely clear that it wouldn't be a hassle—she was going anyway and wouldn't have to go out of her way.

Our friends Paul and Sarah took a similar approach when they called one evening and told us they were making chicken noodle soup and asked if they could bring us some. Again, they made it clear that it wouldn't be an extra effort, and it would have been pretty hard to say no to chicken noodle soup.

Then there was the evening that our friends Jen and Adam arrived on our doorstep with an extra lasagna they'd made. A whole lasagna! Like Dan does, they'd just shown up. Without being asked, they'd taken it on themselves to make a much-appreciated delivery. Being lactose-intolerant, I never imagined that a lasagna I didn't eat would bring me to tears, but that one did.

You can't go wrong working kind acts into your routine unasked. You're making it easier for the recipient to say yes, and what you're offering just might be the high point of their day. And high points are critical. High points can provide much-needed rejuvenation—the delivery of a $2 cup of coffee can push the reset button and prepare someone for the next round of stress.

My friend Alex Li went further than most when he fit kindness into his weekend routine. He felt compelled to act after hearing that a fellow doctor had had to give up running because of an Alzheimer's diagnosis.

Every day for decades, Wally Lim had run before or after work or, on a long day of seeing patients at a San Francisco hospital, during lunch. He also competed in at least a marathon or two every year. Running was as much a part of his daily life as being a doctor. When Wally was diagnosed with early-onset Alzheimer's disease at fifty-two, he was forced to retire, and although the dedicated healer was devastated, the end of his career only made him that much more determined to hold on to his daily running regimen. Before long, though, he stopped being able to find his way home and he'd be lost for hours. His wife, Linda, even had to call the police a few times to find him. Heartbroken, he was forced to give up another passion.

It was a difficult time for Wally, Linda and their three daughters, one in elementary school, one in middle school and one in high school. Wally would become confused when he was with nonfamily members, and when he and Linda had guests, he would sometimes go up to his room to be by himself because the stimulation was too much for him. As is common with Alzheimer's patients, he would also get angry at times.

"He himself knew he had Alzheimer's and that he couldn't do a lot and couldn't do what he previously could do," Linda says. "It wasn't an easy time for him."

Back at the health center where Wally used to work, Alex had recently taken over as medical director after Wally's successor left. As it had been for Wally, running was as much a part of Alex's life as being a physician. He regularly changed into workout gear to get in weekday runs during lunch, and he competed in races. So when staff members told him about Wally's situation, he felt the full weight of it. As a physician, he knew how heartbreaking an Alzheimer's diagnosis is, and as an endurance athlete, he understood the devastation of not being able to run.

"I put myself in Wally's position," he says. "It would be crushing to lose work and running. It wasn't possible for Wally to return to work, but he *could* start running again, and I thought that would be amazing for him."

Realizing that Wally lived nearby, Alex emailed Linda explaining that he didn't want Wally to have to sacrifice running and would like to run with him on weekends. He also suggested that the rest of the family might benefit from some time to themselves. Grateful for his thoughtfulness, Linda accepted the offer.

When Alex came by to introduce himself and invite Wally to run with him, Wally was clearly thrilled, and he accepted, too.

"The Saturday runs are when Wally got really happy," Linda says. "Wally would get up bright and early and be ready, waiting for Alex."

The runs were at least six miles and usually crossed through San Francisco's Golden Gate Park. Alex also took Wally to compete in a few races.

"Every time Wally came home, he was so happy there was something he could still do when so much was taken away," Linda says.

"He would be smiling and just sweating, dripping, and there'd be a big smile on his face and he'd try to hug me when he was all wet."

All told, Wally and Alex ran more than eight hundred miles together. When Wally eventually started to slow down, Alex continued to show up every weekend and go at Wally's pace. Finally, after four years, the weekend runs came to an end when Alex accepted a job in Los Angeles.

"Running with Wally was great for both of us," he says. "For a moment there, he wasn't Wally with dementia. He was Wally the runner or Wally the physician talking about patient care with a colleague. I could tell it brightened his day and he was always happier after a run. I enjoyed the company and I looked forward to our runs. We had great runs."

"People can ask, 'Can I do something for you?' or say, 'Let me know if you need something,'" Linda says, "but it's hard to ask for help. It's the individual who goes ahead and does something without you asking him that changes your life. Those are the times when it makes the most difference. Alex, being the kind soul that he is, went running with Wally, and Wally could do something he really loved with someone who gave him a lot of patience and respect. Seeing my husband happy meant the world to me."

TALK IS NOT CHEAP

One of the reasons Wally was happiest on Saturdays was the conversation. Even though he wasn't practicing anymore, he got to talk business with a colleague. For those precious hours, he felt like his old self again. People who are going through health crises often experience a shift in perspective that gives them a deep appreciation of simple pleasures like meaningful conversation and chicken noodle soup. Anything that breaks the thought cycle playing in their heads like a broken record—*I feel awful. Will I live? Will my family be okay?*—is likely to be music to their ears. During Mia's treatment, my brother visited us every week, and we'd talk about anything and everything except cancer—Rob's battle with his contractors over home renovations, reminiscences about his twenty-first birthday, the question of whether my athletic skills were more suited to a career as a professional frisbee golfer or a pro wrestler. We talked about nothing that had any relevance to Mia's situation, but it meant everything.

Conversation is medicine that any of us can dispense, and it provides lasting respite. Morning meditation keeps some people balanced for the day, but it didn't work for me; it was hard to get out of my head when everything was quiet. But a good conversation gave me an hour or so of escape that in turn provided me with balance for much of the rest of the day.

The power of simple conversation—of listening—isn't to be underestimated. For health care providers, it's one of the ways they "treat" the whole person. Patients' needs go beyond the purely physical, and the way their emotional needs are met can set the tone for their recovery. In our case, Mia's team always made it clear that she was regarded as a human being rather than just one of many cancer patients—it's hard to convey how much comfort that provided us. For others, careful listening and a thoughtful approach can make the difference between a terrifying situation and one that the patient is able to work through. That's what happened with nine-year-old Josh Wade.

Josh had been having health issues, and his physician ordered testing to see if the problem was celiac disease or something else. As part of the process, Josh had to go in for an endoscopy, and he was nervous about it. His solution: he took his favorite stuffed animal, a wolf named Goldie, to keep him company while he would be under sedation.

In the procedure room, he made fast friends with all the staff on hand and introduced them to Goldie. Everyone played along and generally made both Josh and his father, Kevin, feel comfortable. At one point, though, Josh noticed that he wasn't the only one who needed some medical attention. The wolf had a tear in his leg.

"Daddy, he needs stitches," he said. "Can the doctor fix him?"

Kevin laughed. "Well, I think we should probably wait and give him some stitches at home. There are lots of patients here who need help really soon, and I think he'll probably be okay till we get home. Can we stitch him up at home?"

Josh smiled. "Okay." Then he drifted off to sleep, holding Goldie close.

The endoscopy went smoothly, and he was soon in the recovery room. When Kevin walked in, Josh was still asleep, his little wolf on his stomach—in a leg cast and a surgical mask. When Kevin looked closely, he saw that Goldie's "wound" had been closed with five or six surgical-quality sutures.

The thoughtfulness of the gesture hit Kevin fully when Josh came to. In his first moments of consciousness, instead of focusing on his discomfort, he focused on *his wolf's* condition.

"Daddy, Goldie got stitches."

"How about that?"

"I think he'll be okay."

"I think so, too. I think you'll be okay, too. What do you think?"

Josh nodded bravely. Kevin knew his son's tears were close, but because of the distraction the staff had provided, he had time to ease into the potentially frightening scene he'd woken up to. He had a chance to get used to a situation that felt foreign in every possible way, and he wasn't nearly as upset as he probably would have been without that distraction. Goldie's stitches had made all the difference.

"My tears were close, too, as I thanked the doctors and nurses," Kevin says. "It was such a sweet gesture by busy professionals, and I'll never forget it."

Neither will Josh. It's been six years and he still talks about it today. As for the diagnosis, he does have celiac disease, but he's successfully managing it and leading a healthy and happy life.

"We were both very lucky to be in such caring hands," Kevin says.

WHAT WE CAN DO

You don't have to be a health care provider to care for those in poor health. The people in this chapter provided a range of care from a cup of coffee to the gift of life. If you know someone going through a crisis—and this goes for any crisis, not just a health crisis—keep in mind that their life has undergone an upheaval and that little things like a half hour of your company have probably come to mean more than they used to. At any given time, talking with your brother-in-law about things of no importance whatsoever may be what's needed more than anything else.

Here are some things to keep in mind when you're reaching out with coffee and conversation:

Be present

If you think someone is going through a crisis, you might be inclined to avoid them out of fear of saying the wrong thing or creating an awkward situation. Don't worry about that. Usually, the best thing we can do is to be present. If you think they might not want company, ask.

Consider your greetings

If you know that someone isn't doing well, instead of "How are you?" you can say, "It's great to see you."

Remember to pause

Often, you don't need to say much, especially if a conversation turns serious. Pause for five seconds each time you're going to speak so that the other person has a chance to say more (and so you don't accidentally interrupt). Often, they'll take that opportunity to continue sharing how they're feeling.

Ask first

The person you're talking with needs the space to decide whether to bring up their problems. If you think *you* should bring them up, ask first. It might be the last thing someone wants to discuss.

Avoid giving advice

In most cases, it's good to avoid giving advice unless you're asked. When you're giving advice, you're not spending that time listening to how the other person feels. And trust me, when you're going through a tough time, everyone has advice.

You don't need all the answers

If you don't know how to respond to what someone says, you don't have to say anything. You can simply give them a hug. You can also thank them for sharing, which people greatly appreciate. Or you can say, "I'm here for you," or, if appropriate, you can ask, "How can I help?"

Don't try to identify with someone

It's natural to try to identify with others—"I know how you feel," "My mom had the same problem," etc.—but it often comes off wrong because everyone's experience is different and the other person wants you to appreciate their unique situation. (And for some strange reason, in the case of cancer, those unrelated stories often end up with the person in question dying.) While writing this book, I spoke with hundreds of people in difficult circumstances, and after "Be present," this was the most frequent suggestion I heard.

Don't find the silver lining

We want to make things better, so it's natural to try to find a silver lining. Don't. Saying "Everything happens for a reason" or "At least you aren't in Mary's situation" isn't likely to be helpful. Instead, you could say something like "I'm really sorry. It sounds like you're in a lot of pain." You also don't have to tell people that everything will be all right. That might not be true and they know that. Your just being around will be a great comfort.

Engage them in an activity

When you visit, you're usually going to be a welcome distraction. Engage the person in a game or an activity they love.

Be yourself

The person you're planning to see likes you for a reason—so relax, be yourself and schedule a visit.

. . . .

TAKE FIFTEEN MINUTES TO . . .

Add yourself to the worldwide bone marrow registry to save the life of someone like Jay Feinberg. If you live in the United States or Canada, visit the Gift of Life website (giftoflife.org) to sign up. If you live elsewhere, you can use a list of global registries on the World Marrow Donor Association website (wmda.info) to help you become a bone marrow donor.

For information on the bone marrow donation process and organizations dedicated to sharing "the gift of life," from local blood banks to international bone marrow registries, check out page 211 of the Hall of Fame.

. . . .

WORD POWER

"During my second year of nursing school our professor gave us a quiz. I breezed through the questions until I read the last one: 'What is the first name of the woman who cleans the school?' Surely this was a joke. I had seen the cleaning woman several times, but how would I know her name? I handed in my paper, leaving the last question blank. Before the class ended, one student asked if the last question would count toward our grade. 'Absolutely,' the professor said. 'In your careers, you will meet many people. All are significant. They deserve your attention and care, even if all you do is smile and say hello.' I've never forgotten that lesson. I also learned her name was Dorothy."

—JOANN C. JONES
(AS QUOTED ON THE SUSPENDED COFFEES WEBSITE)

I'LL NEVER FORGET the kindness of my grandmother's words. Her letters began arriving regularly after I started my business. I was twenty-two and money was tight, and my wife and I supported ourselves mainly on her minimum-wage restaurant job. She also had an $8-an-hour gig at another restaurant, where she'd arrive at closing time every night and bake cookies in the basement until two in the morning—a time when the area was sure to be deserted. But she never complained. Between the work she did and the meager wages I could sometimes pay myself as I worked feverishly to build a business, we were able to cover the below-market rent my Uncle Steve and Aunt Susie generously charged us for an apartment.

And through it all, Nanny sent letters of support. Yes, in the age of emailing, my grandmother was still a big believer in the power of communicating by way of the U.S. mail.

"I hope things are going well," she might write in one of her weekly letters, and she'd always include restaurant coupons, usually for Boston Market. "I'm sending these because every little bit counts."

We didn't go out to eat often, so we rarely used the coupons, but they were always good for inspiration.

Nanny also sent me newspaper articles and advertisements. I'd get big envelopes stuffed with stories and full-page ads about various technology companies. "Wanted you to see what the competition is up to," her notes would say.

I loved it. I had a fledgling two-person company building websites from my apartment and my grandmother considered me in the same league as Microsoft, Oracle and IBM. Her notes always made me smile.

Later, when I worked for Microsoft, any story that appeared about the company wound up in my mailbox. She'd underline every mention of Microsoft "to make sure you don't miss the important parts." She wanted me to know everything going on in my company so that "your bosses will know how smart you are and you can get promoted." And I have to admit that one of those articles did make me look great in the eyes of our business-unit CEO. He called me out of the blue to ask a technology question one day, and thanks to a story Nanny had sent, I knew the answer!

As our family shared memories of Nanny at her memorial service several years ago, I was surprised to hear all the other grandkids mention the coupons and personal clippings she'd sent them. I'd had no idea she was sending them to all of us. As my cousin Richard put it, "There were nine of us, and every one of us thought we were her favorite."

Nanny's notes weren't profound or more than a sentence or two, but they came from her heart. Some of my most powerful memories of her have to do with the five minutes she'd take to send me those notes and clippings. Over a decade later, I still have some of the coupons. Although they expired long ago, the one hanging in my office hasn't lost its power to make me smile.

A FEW GOOD WORDS

Words provide us with an amazing opportunity. Whether we spend five minutes and fifty-five cents to drop someone a line or make a greater investment, there's no limit to the impact our words can have. We can express love, brighten a day and transform lives. My friend Luis Olivieri tells the story of a teacher whose words of encouragement changed everything for him.

He was in eleventh grade at Jose de Diego High School in Mayaguez, Puerto Rico, and just wanted to live in the moment. He considered college to be something outside his abilities and his reach.

"I never saw myself as someone intelligent, and I certainly didn't see myself as university-student material," he says. "I didn't have any clue to what was going to happen with my life. I figured I'd be a salesman in a store somewhere like my grandfather, my father and my older brother."

After a science exam one day, his teacher Victor Casiano dismissed the rest of the class but asked Luis to stay. Luis assumed he was in trouble for something.

When the others had left, the teacher leaned back in his chair. "What are you doing wasting your time and wasting my time?" he said.

What?

"You are one of the smartest kids in the class. You should be focused and thinking about going to college. You should work harder in school."

Luis didn't say anything. "You just listen during those 'open your eyes' moments," he says. "This was coming from someone I really respected, so it was important. Listening to Victor telling me I could succeed was a very powerful moment."

It was a turning point, in fact. Before that conversation, although he'd excelled in science, he'd barely gotten by in his other classes because he just didn't care about those subjects. But afterward, he started taking them seriously and getting better grades. Science remained first in his heart, though, and he teamed up with Victor and another teacher on science projects that they'd work on during class, after school and on weekends. Victor also encouraged him to participate in science fairs. Luis was skeptical about his chances, but he went on to win at the local, municipal and regional levels for a project on the distribution of lichens—which is a barometer of pollution—in the western region of Puerto Rico.

It was too little too late, though. Although he also went on to do well on the college boards, his lackluster start to high school dragged his GPA down low enough that he wasn't accepted to the University of Puerto Rico even though he'd applied to the Mayaguez campus for agronomy, which had the lowest GPA requirement. Unfortunately, it was the University of Puerto Rico or nothing because his parents couldn't afford to send him to a private school.

Victor had instilled Luis with too much self-confidence to accept the verdict quietly, so he met with the university admissions director. She wasn't budging, though.

"Honey, if you do not have the GPA, you cannot get in," she told him.

As definitive as that sounded, he didn't give up. When he saw the chancellor outside the admissions office, he asked for five minutes of his time.

"He was this huge tall guy, and he put his arm around my shoulder and walked me to his office. We were standing around his conference table and I opened my small suitcase and started taking out the science awards and putting them on the table. I had the certificates framed and there were a couple of medals. It was very casual conversation, and he asked a lot of questions: 'What is this award for? Can you tell me about your project?' When he had no more questions, I waited."

"You know your work says more about you than your GPA," the chancellor finally said. "I'm going to give you a chance to come to the university."

"I was about ten feet tall," Luis says. "We went to the admissions director, who told me I couldn't get in, and he said, 'I want this guy in,' and he signed the paperwork right there."

Luis graduated in 1992 with a bachelor of science degree and later received a master of science. Today, he works at Hopeworks, a nonprofit organization that provides education and training in technology and entrepreneurship. Its goal is to break the cycle of poverty and violence among youths in Camden, New Jersey—one of America's poorest cities and often cited as one of the most dangerous. An expert in geographic information systems, Luis could be earning top dollar at a consultancy, but it's more important to him to help youths.

"It's a lot like what Victor did for me. His words of encouragement after a science test made me believe in myself. At Hopeworks, I'm helping young people understand their potential and helping them understand that they can do way more than they think they can do."

THAT WAS QUITE AN INTRODUCTION

It may be no surprise that the words of a teacher or any mentor can have the kind of impact they had on Luis, but even the words of strangers can change a life. For Ricardeau Scutt, it was a taxi passenger's words that put him on the path to the American dream.

"In Haiti, a job is like winning the lottery," says Ricardeau, whose father brought him to Philadelphia in 2000 to improve his chances of finding employment. But Ricardeau, who was twenty at the time, spoke little English, and he didn't have any more luck than he'd had in Haiti. The months rolled by, but the offers didn't roll in.

His father, who spoke English, had found work as a cabdriver, though, and he happened to mention Ricardeau's struggles to a passenger. It was just a conversation like he might have with anyone, but it planted a seed.

"The guy told my dad to bring me and meet him Monday morning outside an office building in Center City, Philadelphia," Ricardeau says. "The stranger introduced me to his friend, who was the boss of a Saladworks. I got hired on the spot as a dishwasher."

Ricardeau worked hard at Saladworks, studied English in his free time and even took on a second job. A year and a half later, he earned a position as weekend assistant manager at the franchise, and the following year he was named general manager. His store did so well financially and had such a good customer-satisfaction record that the Saladworks executives often used it as the model to show to potential franchisees. A company vice president even asked him to appear in a video to be used for training new managers.

But Ricardeau wasn't interested. "No, thank you," he emailed back.

A week later, CEO John Scardapane wrote him. "Can you help out?"

"No, thank you," Ricardeau answered. But this time he explained himself. "I don't speak English well enough."

Then he got another email from the CEO. "Basically, he said, 'Don't be an idiot,'" Ricardeau says. "So I told him that if my boss is okay with my participation, I would do it." That was at 11:10. At 11:20, Ricardeau got a phone call from his boss and agreed to participate in the video.

Before Ricardeau headed to New York City for the shoot, though, Scardapane asked him to make a stop at a New Jersey Saladworks and serve as manager for a day. It turned out to be quite a day.

For starters, one customer paid for $28 worth of food in mostly pennies while the line behind him grew ever longer. At one point, the man became flustered and dropped many of those pennies. "I could see that the customer probably had some special needs, so I moved him to another register so I could help him while the other employees helped the other customers," Ricardeau says. At the end of the transaction, the customer tried to tip him, but Ricardeau graciously refused.

Later, a chaperone accompanying ten senior citizens told Ricardeau that they needed to have their food in hand within ten minutes or they'd be late for a bingo game. While the Saladworks team took orders from the seniors, who clearly loved to talk over each other, a food fight broke out among some college students in the store. In response, a mall cop on a Segway rode in and started zipping around saying "beep beep" to customers who were in his way and doing little else beyond adding to the chaos. Obviously, Ricardeau was on his own here.

Ultimately, he managed to get the food fighters to leave and saw to it that the senior citizens' orders were completed twenty seconds before their chaperone started blowing the whistle he'd brought to herd his charges out the door, whether they'd gotten their food or not.

After his shift, the store's video camera captured Ricardeau saying with a smile, "It's a nice day in America."

The next day, Ricardeau traveled to New York, where he and three other top managers from across the county got a big surprise. Scardapane informed them that the training video had been a ruse. All of them had been filmed with hidden cameras while working at the same New Jersey store, and the chaos they'd all encountered had been perpetrated by actors who'd been told to give the managers the toughest shifts of their lives.

Why would Saladworks do this to its favorite managers? Did Scardapane just have a lousy sense of humor? Did he *enjoy* pushing his top people to their emotional limits?

The truth, he informed the managers, was that they'd been participating in a competition for ownership of a franchise—a competition Ricardeau had won.

"I almost cried," Ricardeau says. "Sixteen years earlier I had no job. I started as a dishwasher, and that day I became the owner of a Saladworks. This is the American dream."

Married with five children, Ricardeau now runs the business with his wife—whom he'd met at Saladworks—and two of his children work there. Besides allowing him to support his immediate family, his Saladworks career has enabled him to support family members still living in Haiti—all of it made possible by an introduction from a stranger.

And Ricardeau has a message for that stranger: "From the bottom of my heart, I would like to say, 'Thank you.' Me and my entire family here and in Haiti appreciate what you did for me. If I see you again, I will give you a big hug. You changed my life and my entire family's life. You literally put me in the position I am in."

The stranger also inspired Ricardeau to use that position to help others. "He is my model. Every day I do one good deed. I use my business as a way to help someone out daily. Whether it's a homeless person or a cop. Once a day, everyone should do something nice for someone. I'm living proof that you never know who you're going to help and how big of a difference it is going to make."

TWO LITTLE WORDS

No one is more familiar with the power of words than my friend Cheryl Rice. She needs only two words to open channels between people in a profound way. It began when she was working on a work project that had her so frustrated and upset that she couldn't sleep at night. Finally, a colleague gave her a card on which were printed just two words, but they were the perfect words: "You Matter."

Cheryl teared up when she read the message. "I've struggled at times with my own self-worth, and when I received the card, it felt as if a question I carry around with me had been answered. I matter. That expression from her to me filled me up."

She was so touched by the gesture that she ordered a hundred of her own cards to give away, first to family and friends and then just to acquaintances. Eventually, she also started leaving cards in strategic locations to brighten strangers' days—in the credit card holders at gas pumps, in library books, on windshields.

And then she got bolder.

She was standing in a checkout line one day behind a woman of about sixty. When the cashier asked her how she was, the woman said, "Not so good. My husband just lost his job and my son is acting out. The truth is, I don't know how I'm going to get through the holidays." Then she handed her food stamps to the cashier.

"My heart ached," Cheryl says. "I wanted to help but didn't know how. Should I offer to pay for her groceries? Ask for her husband's résumé? I did nothing, and the woman left the store."

As Cheryl walked into the parking lot, she spotted the woman returning her shopping cart and remembered something in her purse that might help her. Her heart pounded as she approached the woman.

"Excuse me," she said. "I overheard what you said to the cashier. It sounds like you're going through a really hard time. I'd like to give you something." And she handed her a "You Matter" card.

When the woman read it, she began to cry. "You have no idea how much this means to me," she said through her tears and hugged Cheryl.

"I hadn't anticipated her reaction," Cheryl says, "and when I walked back to my car, I cried, too."[5]

It was such a powerful experience that she wanted to share it. For her final project in her applied positive psychology certificate program in 2016, Cheryl decided to ship sets of thirty "You Matter" cards free to anyone who signed up online and agreed to share this message with others. She called her project the You Matter Marathon.

"If I hadn't had a card, I don't know that I would have gone up to that woman and said anything," she says. "Cards can give us permission to do this. This is what it's all about—seizing these moments of our common humanity and relating to each other as human beings. I wanted other people to have this experience."

Recipients say the cards have changed their lives. A woman named Sandy wrote Cheryl with this story:

When I gave my grown son a "You Matter" card, he was fighting to hold back tears. He simply held it and looked at it for about a minute. There was a change in his body language, and I got a sense that he finally believes that he does matter in my life and is loved. We were finally able to have a meaningful conversation.

The reason it made such a difference in both our lives is because of his past. He suffered from depression for many, many years and kept it well hidden. He had two suicide attempts. I see him every few weeks and we have been trying to mend our relationship. It has been a long process.

But there has been a shift in our relationship since giving him the "You Matter" card. He has always been a very quiet, shy person who has difficulty sharing his thoughts. Now he is opening up more. . . . The "You Matter" card was the link I needed to reach him.

The cards tend to change givers' lives, too. Julie, another Marathon participant, wrote:

Having the "You Matter" cards ready to hand out has caused me to look at people differently. It's hard for me to approach strangers, so this is an opportunity for growth. I try to find people with whom I can have a meaningful interaction. Consequently, I am really looking at people. . . . This is making me a much more connected human.

Which is exactly the idea. "The givers of the cards make this acknowledgement of others a part of their way of being," Cheryl says. "With or without the cards. With eye contact, common courtesy, letting someone cut in line, a few kind words. These are training wheels, and at the end my hope is that people are changed."

The idea has caught on. The You Matter Marathon—no running

required—is in its fourth year, and more than a million cards have been given out in all fifty states and seventy-three countries.

A CALL THAT CHANGED IT ALL

Cheryl's "You Matter" cards demonstrate words' broad array of powers. From strengthening a connection between mother and son to *creating* connections between strangers, words can be amazing agents of change. Besides changing lives, they can go a step further and *save* lives. For a homeless man named Mike, words as humble as "How are you?" were all it took.

Then twenty, Mike had left home to escape the angry tirades of his alcoholic mother thinking he'd be able to find a place to stay within a couple of days, but he was wrong. Even his father, whom he tracked down and met for the first time, wasn't willing to help. So with only a blanket and the clothes on his back, Mike ended up living under one of the bridges across from the Wells Fargo Center in south Philadelphia.

For the next year, he spent his days walking around on tired feet looking for food in trash cans and his nights sleeping under the bridge. He'd officially joined the ranks of "the invisible"—the homeless—and he got used to being ignored.

But that all changed one morning when someone noticed him. There was construction going on in the area, and a worker approached as Mike sat under the bridge.

"Are you okay?" the man asked.

"Yeah, I'm fine," Mike said.

"Do you want something to eat?"

"No, I'm cool."

Being paid attention to was a new experience, and he was wary. But the construction worker was persistent, talking to him for about a half hour and repeatedly inviting him to the work site for some food. Finally, on feet that had become downright painful by now, Mike hobbled to the trailer where the workers took breaks. They talked awhile longer—mostly about Mike's health and the situation with his mother—and Mike had a burger before going back to the bridge.

The next day, the police showed up to check on him—another first. And when they noticed the shape his feet were in, they took him to the hospital. On the way, Mike realized that the construction worker must have made the call. And it was fortunate that he had—at the hospital, physicians told him that his feet were infected and that he would have died if he'd come in much later. As it was, the infection had spread to his ankles, and part of one foot had to be amputated.

While in the hospital and going through rehabilitative therapy for several months, Mike met volunteers from Project HOME, a nonprofit that provides housing to people experiencing homelessness. When his rehab was finished, Project HOME gave him a place to stay in one of their buildings, and he quickly became involved in a full schedule of volunteer activities, including serving on the residents council, starting a Bible study group and joining Project HOME's speakers bureau. He also started a monthly movie night for residents. They hold discussions afterward, and Mike says it's been a bonding experience for everyone. He's also volunteered at the Free Library of Philadelphia and Kairos House, a Project HOME facility, and spoken to students at Saint Joseph's University about his experiences.

When he meets people living on the streets, he always stops and talks to them, and he gives them money when he can. "I've been there and it almost killed me, so I try to never ignore someone in need," he says. "I want to help any way I can."

Mike hasn't had to live on the streets in the twenty years since the construction worker called the police, but he's never forgotten what it's like to be homeless, and he's never stopped being grateful to the man who noticed him.

"I'm still here because of him," Mike says. "I am who I am because of him. I wasn't supposed to be alive right now, but with the blessing of that construction worker, I'm doing it."

WHAT WE CAN DO

We don't need money or an abundance of time to make a difference. We wield incredible power with our words. Think about people you might be able to help just by making an introduction, finding out what's going on in their lives or letting them know you're pulling for them.

A favorite example of mine is a story that appeared online about a woman and her son with autism. They had recently moved into a new apartment complex, and she was nervous because her son was nonverbal and would sometimes throw loud tantrums. How would the neighbors feel about her and her son? Would they give them dirty looks? Talk about them behind their backs? Something worse? Before long, a neighbor asked her to come over, and she was afraid of what she was going to hear. Were they being a nuisance? Was she going to get a lecture? As it turned out, the neighbor gave her a bouquet of flowers with a note saying that *all* the neighbors could see how hard she was working to be a great mom and that they were there to help. The woman felt relief and enormous gratitude, and afterward she could look back at that note any time she needed strength.

Here are some ideas for using your word power for good:

If you have something nice to say, say it

"If you were going to die soon and had only one phone call you could make, who would you call and what would you say? And, why are you waiting?" An excellent question worth asking yourself from author and poet Stephen Levine.

Send "You Matter" cards

Get your thirty free "You Matter" cards and give them out. And by the way, "free" is 100 percent free—no shipping or other charges. The cards are the size of a standard business card. Visit the You Matter Marathon website (youmattermarathon.com) to claim yours.

Lead a group appreciation activity

The late Sister Helen Mrosla, who was a teacher in Minnesota, created this powerful group activity:[6] Give each member of your family, office team, class or other group sheets of paper or note cards with each group member's name written on a different sheet or card. Tell each member to write what they appreciate about the others on that person's sheet/card. The leader then collects all the sheets/cards and gives each member the comments that were made about them. Helen said her ninth-grade students were always surprised in a positive way. She discovered just how meaningful this activity could be when she attended the funeral of a former student, a soldier killed in the line of duty. His parents shared that their son had taken his sheet of compliments with him when he was deployed, and other former students added that they, too, still cherish the sheets.

You can work this activity into a family tradition or holiday like Thanksgiving. At Big Brothers Big Sisters (BBBS) and the Ronald McDonald Camp (RMC), a camp in the Poconos for kids with cancer where I've been a volunteer, we've done something similar. BBBS employees each have a board where colleagues post notes saying what they appreciate about a different employee every few weeks. At RMC, the counselors wrote notes to each other at the end of camp sharing what they appreciated. I know RMC staff members who still have their notes from a decade ago!

Share your stories

When my grandfather died, I learned a lot of wonderful things about him. At age ninety-two, Popop decided to start working out again and got a gym membership (thankfully, at a gym attached to a hospital), and after he died I learned from his trainer that he was a favorite with members because he would cheer on everyone at the gym. At his memorial service, the owners of the restaurant where he'd had pizza once a week told me that when Popop visited, they'd catch him picking up stray trash, and he always asked the staff how they were doing and about their children. It meant a lot to hear these kinds of stories at Popop's funeral. Now I share anecdotes and memories with friends who have lost loved ones, and it's been appreciated.

Write to people you don't know

Support people you don't know with cards and letters. In most cases, you send the letters to organizations that then forward them to the recipients. On page 213 in the Hall of Fame section, I list thirteen organizations that will deliver your letters of encouragement to kids in the hospital, women newly diagnosed with breast cancer, troops on the front lines, children in foster care, refugees and others who could benefit from your support.

. . . .

TAKE FIFTEEN MINUTES TO . . .

Say thanks. List the people you're thankful for, and once you're done, pick one person to write to and tell them why. A note will take as little as ten minutes of your time, but the recipient will probably keep it forever. Why not set aside fifteen minutes a week for writing these notes? (On his birthday, my friend Mike sends a quick note of thanks to one person for each year he's been alive. That's a great way to appreciate all you have in your life and make other people's day. That said, for some of us, one letter for every five years we've been alive might be more reasonable.)

. . . .

CHAPTER

JUST SAY YES

"My son's school has a strict 'no hats' policy, but they of course made an exception for a little girl who had cancer and lost her hair due to chemo. I was really impressed when I got a notice from the school that a group of fifth graders made a deal with the principal that anybody who wanted to wear a hat on Fridays could—as long as they donated $1 to cancer research. So far they've raised almost $500 between all the grades."
—MELODY W., DES MOINES, IOWA
(FROM THE WEBSITE CAFEMOM)

WHILE SERVING A four-year prison sentence, Julius Patterson focused on his future. Almost every day, he taught a cognitive behavioral psychology class on decision-making to about seventy inmates. It was a win-win: he was helping them and gaining experience that might translate to a job. Meanwhile, he sent multiple letters to Hopeworks, where I volunteer, asking if we'd have a place for him in our job training program when he was released. He also had his sister and his parole officer check to make sure we'd have a spot. We assured them all that we would.

And when the time came, we did. After completing our training program, Julius successfully interviewed for an internship with a business we run that coaches organizations in how to help people who have experienced trauma. He went on to train Camden City School District employees and local company executives.

Julius was also a student in my Hopeworks entrepreneurship class. Knowing how many young people leave prison only to return months later, he dreamed of starting a nonprofit to help former inmates succeed, and in the meantime, he started searching for a job where he could develop his skills as a social worker. But his search wasn't easy. Many employers won't hire you if you're a former inmate, and after years of incarceration, you don't have a network to support you. Those are two of the reasons why 83 percent of people released from state prison wind up getting arrested again—no job and no hope.[7]

But Julius kept at it and made it to the final round of interviews with a nonprofit where he could begin a career of helping others. As it turned out, the agency was comfortable with his criminal record and loved his attitude and experience, but he hadn't graduated college and the position required a four-year degree.

Many companies require a college degree not because it's an indication that a prospective employee is competent but because that's just the way it's done. Julius had just become the latest victim of the way it's done.

But he asked the company to reconsider, and the manager told him she'd get back to him. Finally, after a few days that felt much longer, the company informed him that it had made a decision: it would hire him as long as he worked toward a degree.

Julius couldn't have been happier to accept those terms.

It would have been safer for the manager to hire someone who met the standards—if things didn't work out, it wouldn't be because she'd gone around protocol. But fortunately for Julius, when his prospective boss realized that the criteria weren't quite right, she and the other managers decided to say yes instead.

Julius is a fantastic guy—smart, personable and hardworking. In my class, he always volunteered to help his peers, and he had great advice for them. If I still had my business, I'd hire him in a second. But coming out of prison, his options were limited until he got that "yes." And that "yes" was great news both for Julius and for the thousands of people whose lives he'll change when he's running his own nonprofit one day. Meanwhile, he earned a promotion after just six months, and he mentors former inmates in his free time.

Hopeworks has been the setting for lots of stories like this. Another one also involves a former student of mine. A talented marketer, designer and entrepreneur, Caloua Zhané grew up in poverty, responsible for supporting herself and her siblings as a teenager. After graduating high school with a 4.0, she worked seven days a week—at a restaurant, in Hopeworks' job training program, and for her own freelance design business. But even with three jobs, she earned too little to cover her bills or save enough for a security deposit and first month's rent, so she lived on a relative's couch. The path that would move her life forward was anything but clear.

Caloua would have taken any job that would provide financial freedom, but she craved a job related to her passion for digital marketing. A job that offered a reasonable schedule and enough money for her to finally have a stable life and begin college. But she didn't know anyone in digital marketing and, like many teenagers in Camden, didn't have family members who could provide guidance. Fortunately, Hopeworks has volunteers who offer our young people career advice and conduct mock interviews with them. Some of those volunteers are employees at digital marketing agency Seer Interactive, and once they met Caloua, one thing led to another and she was invited to apply for an internship. After getting it and proving herself, she applied for a job, and now she's a part-time Seer employee by day, a college student by night and a freelance designer in between. She earns enough money to cover stable housing, and she's gained enough financial freedom to start saving.

A Seer employee said yes to providing a mock interview, the company said yes to giving Caloua a chance and her life was changed in an instant.

Saying yes to others can make all the difference. Besides helping people like Julius and Caloua get a start in life, it can change the world for a homeless teen or even lead to a scientific breakthrough that will save more lives than we can guess at. And when we say yes to *ourselves*, we can give ourselves permission to open doors that others can follow us through.

OPENING A DOOR TO SUCCESS

When Colleen Landy was program director of Philadelphia's Covenant House shelter for homeless youths, she asked the CEO of the Saxbys Coffee chain for help in "mainstreaming" residents by finding them jobs.

He jumped.

"I told Colleen I'd be there the next morning, and I told her to have the most hirable person ready for me," Nick Bayer says.

When he arrived, high school senior Dante Wilson was ready for him. Dante's mother had kicked him out of the house for running with the wrong crowd and generally behaving irresponsibly. Now that he'd had a taste of life in a homeless shelter, he was desperate to get out.

Nick recounts his first impression: "I get there, look in the window of this little conference room in the shelter and Dante is sitting in a room by himself in a blazer, smiling. You go in thinking it will be a sad place, and there's a young man by himself with a huge smile on his face. I knew I was going to hire him."

Specifically, he hired Dante for his café in Philadelphia's Rittenhouse Square. Dante didn't have job experience, though, so he started with cleaning the café and busing tables. A week later, Nick called his franchisee to see how things were going with Dante.

"It's going really well," he was told. "He's eager, he works hard and he gets along with everybody. By the way, if you don't mind, we'd like to put him through barista training."

So Dante became a barista, and a month later the team created a "team member of the month" award just to show their coworker how much they appreciated his work ethic. Dante wound up winning the award seven months straight.

In his seven years at Saxbys, Dante has been promoted multiple times, and Nick says customers regularly send the company emails singling him out for praise—not a common phenomenon in the coffee-shop industry.

Jobs change lives. When Nick hired Dante, he changed Dante's life. It's a day Dante will never forget. "Mr. Nick Bayer walked into Covenant House and I saw this tall slicked-back-hair, done-up guy and thought, 'I won't get the job,'" he says. "But I got it, and once Saxbys became part of my life, everything happened."

In the wake of Dante's success, Nick has hired many other young people who might otherwise have found it challenging to get jobs.

"I want to make an impact in the city," he says. "It breaks my heart to see young people sleeping on the streets and a fifteen-year-old sticking a gun in someone's face for money. Kids surrounded by bad circumstances see no hope. Now I can do something about that and I'm going to continue to do something about that. I don't want to do the easy thing—I want to do the right thing. We employ seven hundred people, and most of those jobs are entry-level. We can make an effort to hire people who need help for some of those positions. We can teach life skills. My responsibility as a business leader is to be additive and provide them with opportunity and hold them accountable. If they do well, they'll be promoted here, or we'll give them great references so they can succeed somewhere else."

A key way that Saxbys offers life-skills instruction is through its mentoring program. "Some of the kids coming out of challenging circumstances need to be treated a little bit differently than other employees," Nick says. "They need to learn how to show up on time, how to plan time to get from where they are to work, how to use a paycheck properly." Saxbys takes the time to teach those things.

Once a mentee, Dante is now taking a lead in the mentoring program to help guide youths who have come from difficult situations like he did. Considering his level of gratitude for the opportunity that Nick gave him, his commitment to giving back is no surprise.

"Saxbys changed my perspective and my world," he says. "If it weren't for Nick, I'd probably still be living on the streets. To this day, I'm like 'Oh my God, I'm the luckiest guy in the world.'"

CITIZEN SCIENTIST

By hiring a homeless teen, Nick was taking a risk—a risk he's since taken many times. Once, he hired Megan, a student of mine who was homeless and desperately needed a job. I knew Nick from our time volunteering together at Big Brothers Big Sisters, and when I called him, he found her a position, no questions asked. He took a risk to give her the chance she needed, and it helped her turn her life around. Today, Megan is independent and self-sufficient and has her own business that employs others.

Megan and Dante are great examples of why we should take chances on teens. And Jack Andraka is another. If no one had taken a chance on him, countless people would have paid a price.

After a friend of Jack's died of pancreatic cancer, he couldn't stop thinking that things could have been different if the disease had been detected earlier. From researching pancreatic cancer, he knew that almost all patients are diagnosed so late that only the outliers have a chance of survival. There had to be a better way. Specifically, there had to be a better diagnostic test, he believed, and rather than wait for science to come up with one, he decided to do it himself—despite the fact that he was only fourteen.

It was crazy. Jack was a smart kid and passionate about science, but in a lot of ways he was also just a typical teenager. He liked to spend his time mountain biking and kayaking with his friends, and he was a devoted fan of *Glee* and *Family Guy*. What made him think he could come up with a diagnostic test better than what scientists and billion-dollar pharmaceutical companies had already developed?

"Teenage optimism," Jack says now.

And he knew just where to look for help. "I went online to a teen-ager's two best friends: Google and Wikipedia."

After poring through countless online science journals, he found an article that listed eight thousand proteins found in patients with pancreatic cancer. It was a gold mine of possibilities. If he could find a protein that appeared early in the course of the disease, there was hope for an early-detection system.

"And so I'm just plugging and chugging through this gargantuan task," Jack says, "and finally, on the four thousandth try, when I'm close to losing my sanity, I find the protein." It was a protein that's highly elevated in the very early stages of pancreatic cancer cases, when there's still a good chance of beating the disease. It looked like the early biomarker he'd been searching for.

Translating that information into a reasonable test to detect the protein was going to be a challenge, but he was excited to get started. Then something suddenly occurred to him: his kitchen counter hadn't exactly been designed for cancer research. So he decided to apply for a lab position.

Using the wealth of information he'd gathered online, he wrote a proposal for the development of a better test for pancreatic cancer, a tool he hoped would be more effective and less costly than what already existed. Then he sent the proposal off to the two hundred university professors who seemed most likely to offer him support.

"I sat back waiting for these positive emails to come pouring in saying, 'You're a genius! You're going to save us all!'" Jack says before breaking into a laugh. "Then reality took hold, and over the course of a month I got 199 rejections out of those two hundred emails. One professor even went through my entire procedure, painstakingly, and said why each and every step was, like, the worst mistake I could ever make."

Then Jack got his two hundredth response. It was a "maybe."

"It's not every day that you get an email from a fifteen-year-old that comes with a detailed protocol with methods and supplies and what pitfalls you might run into," Dr. Anirban Maitra, professor of pathology, oncology, and chemical and biomolecular engineering at Johns Hopkins School of Medicine, said later in an interview with *CBS News.* "And I said, 'Maybe I will get you a corner in my lab and we will have one of the postdoc fellows supervising you and let's see where all this goes.'"

After an in-person interview, "maybe" became "yes." Maitra offered Jack space, and Jack took full advantage of the opportunity, working at the lab after school every day, on weekends and over holidays.

"I discovered that my 'brilliant' procedure had something like a million holes in it," Jack says. And along the way, there was a lot he had to learn—from the names of tools (he'd initially referred to forceps as "tweezers") to the use of scientific equipment (he caused at least one lab explosion)—but he didn't relent.

The result of his dedication is a diagnostic test that's four hundred times more sensitive than the previous test. It detects pancreatic cancer in its earliest stages, and estimates are that the test will cost only a few cents to produce (more than twenty-thousand times less expensive than today's tests). It's still being perfected, and once it's ready, surviving cancer will become a possibility for countless people who otherwise would have had no hope. There are also plans to use variations of the test for detecting ovarian and lung cancers and—Jack's greatest hope—potentially any disease.

"Hopefully, one day we can all have that one extra uncle, that one mother, that one brother, sister—we can have that one more family member to love."[8]

ASSISTANCE ON REGISTER 3

Sometimes saying yes is simply about helping someone get through the day or the week. During a highly stressful time in my life, I was going to take a trip with my brother and called him the day before.

"Please bring your bathing suit," I said.

"Why?"

"I'm extremely stressed and I need to swim."

"Okay."

No more questions asked. Knowing I didn't want to talk about the situation, he didn't push it, and during the trip he dutifully went swimming with me for hours every day—sometimes at crazy times like 6 a.m. In the end, I didn't have the nervous breakdown I feared, and I believe the "therapy" my brother indulged me in had everything to do with that.

In Kim Grandinette's case, she just needed someone to let her three-year-old son, Paulie, scan coupons at the grocery store so they could get through another day of missing the rest of their family.

Her other son, one-year-old Remington, was in the hospital for the seventh time for breathing problems, and Paulie was struggling with being apart. The fact that Christmas was coming made the separation harder.

"Paulie never let much time pass before reminding me how sad he was that we couldn't be with Bubby [his word for brother] and Daddy, who was staying at the hospital," Kim says.

On the third day of Remington's latest hospitalization, Kim and Paulie stopped by the grocery store and Paulie asked if they could pick out something for his brother "to keep him company and make him happier."

Kim held back her tears. "Sure. What do you think would be something Remy would like?"

They went to the baby aisle and picked out a small stuffed animal, and to cheer Paulie up, Kim bought him a Transformers toy. As they checked out, Paulie told Kristen, the cashier, about the Transformer he was getting because his bubby was in the hospital.

The cashier gave Kim a kind look, and Kim explained the situation.

"I understand what you're going through," Kristen said. "My mom has been sick a lot around the holidays the last couple of years."

As she scanned the groceries, Paulie looked on with interest.

"Ma'am, can I help you?" he said.

Kristen smiled. "Sure." Then she came around the counter to lift him out of the cart, and holding him on her hip, she continued with the checkout. "This is how you scan a coupon," she said. "This is called a bar code, and it has to be facing down like this." She swept it across the register and handed it to him. "Now you can put it right here," she said, pointing to the top of the register, where he proudly deposited it.

"Paulie had never asked to help before," Kim says, "and I'm not sure why he asked that day, but it was obviously important to him and made him *feel* important. As we left, he couldn't stop grinning."

A few minutes later, he was still grinning as she buckled him into his seat in the car. "Mommy, that's fun," he said. "I want to be a cashier when I grow up."

It was a brief moment of happiness during a rough few days. Seeing him smile like that at a time when his world had been turned upside down yet again, Kim was filled with gratitude for Kristen's simple act of kindness.

It's been over a year since that trip to the grocery store, and Remy is better now. As for Paulie, no matter how long Kristen's line is, he insists on waiting for her so he can scan the coupons. Kim figures it's a small price to pay for a priceless gesture.

FRIENDS WITH FOUR PAWS

As you train yourself to say yes for the sake of others, don't forget to say yes to yourself. The more we hear "no," the less likely we are to remember that we deserve better than that. We can't expect to be any good to other people if we don't take care of ourselves, and sometimes that means giving ourselves permission even when no one else will—*especially* when no one else will.

Karen Shirk's life is a case in point. Employed full time and working toward a master's in social work, she thought the fatigue she was feeling was normal. Aren't all college students exhausted? Then one day while she was walking across campus, she went into respiratory arrest. It turned out that she had myasthenia gravis, a debilitating disease that causes muscle weakness and fatigue, and suddenly life became something very different. The independent, hard-charging twenty-four-year-old on her way to changing the world spent the next seven years dependent on hospital care and home health aides.

And then she read about service dogs. "I really liked the concept," she says. "All my life I was a dog person. I thought it would be fantastic because I was sick of always needing to have a person take care of me. I thought if I got a dog, I wouldn't be so dependent on people. I could be at my apartment by myself."

But every agency where she applied for a service dog rejected her. Eventually, a representative of one of the agencies told her why: most agencies didn't give dogs to people who use ventilators because they were considered too disabled to be integrated back into society. Although Karen used a ventilator only to help her breathe at night, the agencies clearly believed there were better candidates for their dogs.

After seven years, Karen couldn't imagine living this way much longer, and she started skipping morphine pills so she could save enough of them to kill herself. When she told her health aide that she was thinking of giving up, though, the aide had another idea: Karen should get an untrained puppy.[9]

"No way," Karen said. "I won't be able to take care of it. I can't even take care of myself."

"Come on," the aide said. "Let's go look at puppies."

To appease her, Karen looked at puppies with her. But she was adamant that it was only window shopping—as far as she was concerned, that doggie in the window would stay in the window.

"She dragged me from place to place looking at puppies, and I was like, 'No, no thanks, I can't do this,' after every visit."

Until she met Ben.

When she saw the black German shepherd pup, she flashed back to a childhood spent moving from place to place as military families often do. A childhood during which bonds were hard to form and the family's black German shepherd was her best friend. "When Ben looked at me, we had an instant connection and I knew he would be my puppy."

She figured her aide would be the actual caretaker, though, and again the aide had another idea.

"She forced me to go out with Ben," Karen says. "I had become a hermit, and she changed that. Even though I was in a wheelchair, I could still take Ben out, feed him and care for him. I just needed someone to make me take that responsibility."

Training Ben so that she could get her life back became Karen's focus, and as she trained him, the bond between them grew. "From the minute I saw him, I wanted to live. With Ben supporting me, I inched closer and closer each day to being able to do something with my life."

For a year and a half, she trained Ben for several hours a day. She took him to classes at a local dog-training school and then sent him to a more advanced school, where professional trainers took over. They also taught Karen how to continue Ben's training at home.

So by the time Karen's life was on the brink again, Ben was ready. The day she returned home after undergoing open-heart surgery, a malfunction of the device that pumped her medicine left her incapacitated and close to death. When the phone rang, Ben pulled the receiver out of its cradle with his mouth and started barking—that had been part of his training. Karen's father was on the other end of the line and knew something was wrong and called the police. Ben was still barking when they arrived.

If it hadn't been for Ben's actions, Karen probably would have been dead by the time her aide arrived the next morning.

Besides saving her life a second time, Ben made it possible for Karen to return to work nine years after her myasthenia gravis diagnosis. "Ben gave me the confidence to do more, and he could do some things for me like open and close doors," she says. "I wasn't afraid of dropping my keys because he could get them for me. He could retrieve my medical bag with emergency meds in it, give things to people for me, like money to a cashier. I had the same level of mobility as before Ben, but I wouldn't do anything before because I had no way of getting help. I knew I needed to go back to work or life would fade away, and because of the confidence Ben gave me, I knew I could. My first day of being back at work was amazing. It was liberating."

As Karen continued to gain confidence about living with her disease, she thought about all the people who needed service dogs but were being rejected because they didn't meet the criteria. How many other lives could be turned around with service dogs? She decided to do something about the problem: She'd train service dogs for kids because most agencies wouldn't work with kids or would only give them companion dogs for use in the home. Companion dogs are good company, but they aren't trained to help the child or the family.

She started by training two dogs out of her one-bedroom apartment, and thus 4 Paws for Ability was born in 1998. In the first few years, she trained dogs for members of her local community who needed them, but when word got out that 4 Paws for Ability placed dogs with kids and had no minimum age requirement, she got an avalanche of requests from all over the United States and places as far away as Japan, Australia and Germany.

For the next ten years, Karen lived off her social security checks rather than taking a salary. Families who wanted dogs would raise $10,000, which in those years covered the cost of training a dog.

Under the nonprofit's protocol, training starts the day puppies are born, when they begin listening to audio recordings of everything from crying babies to jackhammers to traffic. Also, as part of the regimen, they're touched all over, fingers are put into their mouths and they're taken out in public and exposed to so much that they'll be comfortable in any environment. From there, 4 Paws reviews the needs of each child who will receive a dog and trains it accordingly. One family had a nonverbal child who was prone to running away from their home and didn't know how to get back. Once, he escaped on a night when it was twenty below zero, but thanks to the family's dog, which 4 Paws had trained to track the boy, they were able to find him before he could come to harm.

Some dogs are trained to alert families to the early signs of seizures—a blessing for couples who hadn't slept in the same bed for years because one of them always needed to be with their child in case of a seizure. Other dogs are trained to notice the change in a child's scent that occurs when his or her insulin levels change. Grateful parents report that they no longer have to wake up their children multiple times a night to check insulin levels. And unlike traditional service dogs, which other people are encouraged not to pet, all of 4 Paws' dogs are trained to be social butterflies in order to help kids who are often ignored learn to socialize.

For Noah Foust, a boy with autism, the social aspects of his service dog, Harry, have been a very pleasant surprise. His family got Harry in order to help Noah remain safe and curb his aggressive behaviors, and Harry has succeeded on those fronts and more. "Since Harry started going to school with Noah, he's received his first phone call, birthday party invites and lots of drawings and notes sent home from his classmates," his mother, Cathy Foust, says. "This wasn't something we expected, but it's definitely icing on the cake."

"In the world today, people measure success in dollars," Karen says. "I measure success in the number of happy tears cried over stories from our families about their life with their service dog."

One of her favorites is the story of a seventeen-year-old named Dylan who wrote Karen an email thanking her for his dog, Coffee. Before he got Coffee, he had seizures weekly, if not daily—sometimes more than twenty a day. They would often be so severe that he would wet himself and have to endure the embarrassment that followed. As Dylan wrote, "it was the worst. lord I hated that so much." But thanks to Coffee's training in heading off his seizures, he had only three seizures in his first year with Coffee. "you dont know how happy that makes me," he wrote.

Another life-changing event: Dylan was no longer invisible. The kids at school had never really given him a chance—he and an aide used to sit by themselves in the lunchroom—but now when the kids came over to pet Coffee, they saw Dylan for the smart, funny, kindhearted guy he is. Eventually, Dylan and Coffee found themselves in such demand that they had to move to a bigger table to accommodate all the new friends.

Most exciting of all, Dylan got a date for the prom—a date who asked *him*.

"because of you all this gret stuff is hapening to me," he signed off in his email to Karen. "thank you for giving me coffee i love you."

For almost two decades, 4 Paws for Ability has been changing lives like Dylan's, placing about fourteen hundred dogs in that time. It's the largest agency in the United States devoted primarily to pairing service dogs with kids, and Karen believes it's also the largest in the world. The operation has grown to the point where it places more than a hundred dogs a year. The wait for a placement is about two years, but Karen says her dream is to be able to provide a dog for every child in need within the amount of time it takes to raise and train it—about a year.

Families are now asked to raise $17,000 to help cover 4 Paws' training costs, which amount to $40,000 to $60,000 per dog, and Karen says this also teaches applicants and their families something valuable. Like Karen had been, many disabled people are taught to wait for a handout, she says, but raising money shows them they can help themselves.

It also shows them how many people in the community care about them. Like the health aide who took Karen puppy shopping.

"I had a close friend who refused to watch me die," she says. "She dragged me from place to place looking at puppies, trying desperately to get me to cling to life again and to find the courage to fight for that life. If I saw her again, I'd say, 'Thank you—you created the beginning of a new life for me.'"

And, so far, for fourteen hundred other families as well.

WHAT WE CAN DO

I was driving aggressively—I hate being late. I wouldn't let cars get in front of me, and I think I even cut off a few pedestrians. At the office, I jumped into the elevator, and though I normally try to hold the door for others, this time I might have looked the other way while the door closed. I was making my problem everyone else's problem.

The irony is that I was going to a Big Brothers Big Sisters meeting—a meeting to talk about how to make the world a better place. Something I certainly hadn't been doing on my way there.

I know I'm less likely to be kind and thoughtful when I'm rushing, and that's true of most people. But being aware of my tendency to be less polite when I'm rushing has proved to be helpful. When I realize I've started racing around, I can sometimes stop myself and take a deep breath. I slow down and take thirty seconds to say "hello," be polite, hold open the door or stop to let a pedestrian cross the street. I need a chance to pause, collect myself and behave the way I want to behave.

Saying yes shouldn't mean we take on so many things that we're too busy to be kind. In fact, saying yes often requires slowing down. If Nick Bayer and Anirban Maitra hadn't been willing to slow down, they probably wouldn't have been able to say yes. I'm sure that Nick knew it would take extra time to train a homeless employee and that Dr. Maitra expected the same of coaching a high school scientist, but that didn't stop two extremely busy people from creating opportunities. When we're willing to slow down, we all have the power to say yes to others and ourselves.

Here are some ideas for saying yes and how to say it:

Figure out what you can offer

You don't have to be a social worker to help. At Big Brothers Big Sisters, we've had auto mechanics who provided free repairs to families who couldn't afford them and dentists who did the same with dental care. They called BBBS and asked our organization to refer families in need. What are your skills, and what organization can pair you with people who could benefit from them? Who in your neighborhood could use a hand? If you don't have any ideas, check out the Hall of Fame, where you'll find a number of nonprofits where you can say "yes" through actions as simple as writing a letter or donating $10.

Create opportunities

A surprising number of jobs are limited to people with college degrees, as Julius found out. And in many cases, a college degree isn't actually a good measure of the skills needed for the job—it's a pedigree requirement rather than a skills requirement. For example, for my company's tech hires, we needed people who had specific coding skills, and a college degree wasn't any indication that a programmer had those. Look at the jobs in your company—are there jobs that shouldn't require a college degree? If you run a business unit or you're a hiring manager, let HR know where you're willing to bypass the degree.

By the way, researchers at Harvard University and Gartner, a research and advisory firm, have found that when degree requirements are eliminated, roles are filled more quickly, retention and engagement improve and costs for sourcing and compensating employees are reduced. It also opens up opportunities for jobs and a middle-class life to millions of Latino and African Americans, who are the people most often shut out of opportunities due to degree requirements.[10]

Make it seem easy

I was chatting with one of my students after class and lost track of time. As I pulled out of the school parking lot and into traffic, I realized I'd never make it to Jack's school on time to pick him up, so I called my wife's friend Patty. I apologized profusely for the fifteen-minute notice, but she told me she was happy I'd reached out and said it would be easy to pick Jack up and take him to her house. I'm guessing it wasn't as easy as she said it was, but she made it *seem* easy. I had to ask for a lot of help when Mia was sick, and although everyone came through, some people told me about how much they had to juggle and the hoops they needed to jump through. I learned that it's a gift to simply say, "I'd love to."

Help others to say yes

Sharon, one of the nurses we often saw at chemo, noticed a woman who was having trouble walking and approached her. "Can I walk with you?" she asked. The woman agreed and Sharon held her arm, guiding her to a chair. While watching them, I thought about how much more thoughtful that was than saying, "Can I help you?" Sharon's choice of words didn't imply a *need* for help, which made it easier for the woman to *accept* help. Similarly, instead of saying, "Can I visit and see if I can help with anything?" I can say, "Can I come see you?" Instead of "Do you need me to come to the hospital with you?" I can say, "Can I come to the hospital with you?" Sometimes it's hard to accept help, but we can make it easier by not calling it that.

Say yes to strangers

Meg Garlinghouse, head of social impact at LinkedIn, is often asked to do informational interviews, and because she benefited greatly from these during her own job search, she feels compelled to participate. Out of curiosity, she started tracking the people she'd met with and found that they were very similar to her (they were from her network, after all). She was disappointed—her vision for LinkedIn was to provide economic opportunity for everyone, especially those who weren't born into opportunity or didn't have access to networks and social capital. So she committed to the "+1" approach: for every person she met with from within her network, she would find someone to meet with outside her network who lacked access to social capital and networks. Meg learned the "+1" concept from a colleague who had been helping his daughter find a job after college and realized that if he and the millions of other parents with strong networks would help just one additional student, they could help close our social capital gap.

. . . .

TAKE FIFTEEN MINUTES TO . . .

Think about your own +1 commitment, which can be whatever you want it to be. One résumé review a week, one conversation a month, one mock interview session a year. But the key is to say yes, ideally on some kind of a regular basis, to someone you don't know who could use your help. Opportunities may be closer than you think. Keep your eyes open for people who fit any of the following descriptions:

- Someone who's reached out to you online for career advice.
- A candidate who applied for an entry-level job at your company but didn't get it due to a common error you've seen candidates make. It may be too late to help them to break in at your company, but you can help give them a better shot with the next application process.
- Someone not in your social network who's mentioned that their son or daughter is hoping to apply to a college or enter a career field that you have some knowledge of. You can follow up to see if they'd like to talk to you about it. Same thing if someone who's not in your social circle has mentioned buying a house, adopting a child or anything else you might be able to offer help with.
- Teachers or nonprofit employees, who are likely to know many people who could use your advice and encouragement on a broad range of topics.

You can find excellent opportunities to say yes to people you don't know through the organizations listed in the Hall of Fame coaching section on page 217. These include opportunities to spend a lunch hour talking with an underserved class about your career or a hobby via online video chat, spend an hour on the phone coaching a veteran interested in your career, become a pen pal with a budding scientist, and provide online coaching to a teen in foster care applying to college.

. . . .

7

BE GOOD COMPANY

"Become friends with people who aren't your age. Hang out with people whose first language isn't the same as yours. Get to know someone who doesn't come from your social class. This is how you see the world. This is how you grow."
—RANDOM ACTS OF KINDNESS FOUNDATION FACEBOOK PAGE

BUSINESS WAS BOOMING. Johnson & Johnson had just hired my company as the Internet advertising agency to manage all its search marketing, Universal Studios had hired us to develop creative and marketing campaigns for some of its DVD releases and Hyundai was talking with us about managing online advertising for its U.S. car business.

And with those opportunities came a push from our clients to expand outside Philadelphia and set up offices in Seattle, Los Angeles and other cities where they were headquartered. They wanted us to at least quadruple in size and, in turn, give them better prices. (Part of our business was buying online advertising space, and our clients knew that if we grew exponentially, we would buy more ad space and have more leverage, which would result in lower prices.)

I loved working with our customers, but I didn't want to fly around the country opening and managing multiple offices. It wasn't the lifestyle our management team wanted either. So we set out to find a company that could partner with us or acquire us and provide the scale and offices we needed. We met with a number of interested companies, and after a little more than a year we chose aQuantive. Besides meshing well with our culture and management style, aQuantive gave us scale—it was the biggest Internet advertising agency in the United States.

The week before we closed the deal, there was a flurry of activity. In addition to the constant back-and-forth of redlined versions of contracts, I had to organize hundreds of pages of information that aQuantive needed. On top of that, we were carefully planning the communications to our employees, our clients and the media. I think I slept less than three hours a night that week.

On Friday, the paperwork was signed, and we planned to make the announcement on Monday. I didn't wait that long to tell my grandfather, though. He'd always been my biggest fan, and I wanted him to hear the news before the announcement. During our nightly phone calls, we'd talk about his ideas for my business and discuss what he'd seen on the news and how it related to my company. He'd also give my business cards to people he thought had the potential to become clients. Knowing Popop, I suspected that meant he was on a street corner passing out my cards to everyone he met. Of course, when I told him about the sale, he was thrilled.

On Monday morning, we took our entire company off-site to announce the acquisition. We knew that people are naturally nervous about change, and we wanted everyone in our company to have an opportunity to ask questions and discuss the benefits we'd receive as a part of aQuantive. After the meeting, my assistant approached me with a concerned look. "I think you should listen to your voice mails," she said.

There were three of them, all from Popop. He said that as soon as the stock exchange had opened that morning, he bought a share of the acquiring company. Then he called the company's chief financial officer to let him know he was a stockholder and needed to see the company's financials. The call had gone to voice mail, though, so Popop then called much of the financial staff, but none of them answered their phones either, and nobody returned his calls. He was extremely concerned and asked me to call him immediately. "How can a company get clients if they don't answer their phones at nine in the morning?" he wanted to know. "How will you stay in business? Can you get out of the deal?" He assured me he'd keep making calls until someone answered.

What Popop didn't know was that the company is located in Washington state. He'd left my new bosses messages at 6 a.m. Pacific time.

Hoo-boy.

Popop had always been free about "helping" me. Once when my wife and I were newly married, for example, he offered me tips on how to get her pregnant. Hard of hearing, he shouted instructions regarding my "plumbing" loudly enough to be heard by everyone at the party we were attending. (As you probably realize by now, my grandparents were obsessed with the subject of my having kids.) And I'd get calls from Popop's dentist, among others, whom Popop told to call me because he thought he'd make a great client. That was Popop.

So now, with no idea what he'd said in his messages to my new company's employees, I was a little concerned. I could only imagine what the executives were thinking: *Wait a minute—we just bought this little company run by a kid, and the guy's grandfather is calling us saying he needs to see our books? What the %&#*?* So I left a message for the chief financial officer explaining that my grandfather was my biggest fan and very excitable and that the company should ignore his messages.

I never heard a word from anyone at the company about the voice mails.

I'm smiling as I think about it. We were only one day into the sale to aQuantive and Popop was already keeping tabs on the company to make sure it was well-run. How lucky was I to have a grandfather like that?

During my years with aQuantive, Popop would read every one of our publicly filed hundred-plus-page documents word for word—including footnotes—and he'd highlight every section that he had questions about. Later, after Microsoft bought aQuantive and I became an employee at Microsoft, he constantly offered me advice for keeping my job and getting ahead.

Popop was one of my greatest role models. He made my life so much richer just by being himself—engaged and excited. I didn't need him to be an interesting person (although he was)—I needed him to be interested. And I've made an effort to adopt his enthusiasm. Thinking of Popop reminds me to try to be excited and interested even when I'm exhausted.

I've also had many other mentors who shaped my life. I've been so blessed, in fact, that it always takes me by surprise to hear from organizations like MENTOR: The National Mentoring Partnership, that one in three young people grows up without a single mentor. When you consider that just being ourselves can help someone else through life, it seems impossible that there could be a shortage of mentors. I know there's not a shortage of *potential* mentors, though. If all of us who are capable stepped up, I believe there would be a mentor for everyone. What's a mentor, after all, but someone who's learned something about life and passes it on?

THE DYNAMIC DUO

An organization that finds mentors and facilitates mentorship is Big Brothers Big Sisters. My friend Tom McElvogue was awarded the Big Brother of the Century award by our local chapter in 2015, and when asked what he did to earn it, he humbly says he just showed up a couple of times a month. But in BBBS, the concept of showing up is a big deal. It means adults (Bigs) are fully present—as their authentic selves—with the kids they're matched with (Littles). It means being yourself, like Popop was always himself. And if you're skeptical of the value of that, consider the influence Tom had on his Little in this story.

In the early seventies, Tom was paired with eight-year-old Joe Wootten when he got a call from the CEO of BBBS. "We're getting free advertising space, and we're using real Bigs and Littles in the ads," he said. "If you and your Little are interested, you can come to a screen test at a Philadelphia studio to see if you're a good fit for the ads."

When Tom checked with Joe, he was ecstatic.

"We're gonna be on TV and billboards!" he said. "All my friends will see us. This is gonna be the greatest thing ever!"

Tom tried to rein in his expectations. "Listen, you and I are a great match, but we might not get the part. Very few of the people at the test will be in the ads."

But Joe didn't hear what he was saying. He told Tom he was wrong. He knew they'd be chosen. Tom just hoped his enthusiasm would cool over time.

When the day of the screen test arrived, he drove to Joe's house to pick him up and found him sitting outside waiting. He was wearing nice clothes, his hair was combed and he was ready to go—all unusual for him. When he got into the car, Tom could tell right away that he was a bundle of energy. He literally couldn't sit still. So much for cooling off.

Tom tried again to lower his expectations. "You know, we might not get it. It's just great that they picked us for the screen test, don't you think?"

And again, Joe said he knew that they'd get it—and that he couldn't wait.

The screen test turned out to be low-pressure and a lot of fun, and in the days that followed, whenever Tom talked to him, the first thing Joe would say was, "Did they pick us yet?" And he'd go on to say how cool it was going to be when his friends and family saw him in the ads.

Finally, after a little more than a week, Tom got a call from the CEO.

"We heard back from the ad agency," he said.

"How'd we do?" All Tom could think of was how hard it would be if he had to tell Joe they hadn't been chosen.

"They loved Joe. He's great in front of the camera, and they'd like to put him in the ads."

"That's fantastic."

"One more thing—they didn't think you were photogenic enough, so they want to put him with a different Big for the ad campaign. Is that okay?"

"No problem. I can't wait to tell Joe."

What a relief. All that mattered to Tom was that Joe had made it.

When Tom called him, Joe cut to the chase as usual. "Did you hear yet? Did they tell us we got it yet?"

"Yes—you're going to be in the ads!"

Joe started screaming, and Tom could tell he was jumping up and down. When he calmed down, which took several minutes, Tom told him the rest.

"Just one thing. They said that I wasn't as photogenic as you, so you'll be in the ad with another Big Brother. I'll still be your Big Brother—he'll just be in the ads with you."

There was silence at the other end of the line.

"Joe?"

More silence.

Finally, Joe spoke up. "I'm not going to be in the ads. We're a team, and if you aren't right for the ads, I'm not right for them either."

"Joe, it's completely fine for you to be in the ads without me. I think you should be in the ads."

"No. If they don't want you, they can't get me."

"Are you sure?"

"Yes, we're a team."

Then they shifted to talking about what they were going to do that weekend, and after they hung up, Tom sat on his bed and let the tears come. He was shocked. Joe had been so excited about the prospect of being in the ads that it never occurred to Tom that his absence would be a deal-breaker.

They were even more of a team than he'd realized.

Joe and Tom are still a team. They've built a friendship over decades of everyday get-togethers to watch movies, take part in Cub Scouts and just hang out and talk. Joe was a member of Tom's wedding party in 1973, and they and their families have celebrated Christmas together ever since they connected as Big and Little forty-seven years ago. Joe's mother is so impressed with the effect Tom has had on Joe's life that she donates to BBBS every year to help other "teams" find each other.

Big Brothers Big Sisters has a finely tuned system for facilitating mentoring relationships, and it works wonderfully. After the application process and background checks, adults willing to share their time twice a month are matched with a child. Then BBBS organizes various activities to help matches bond and provides guidance to help the relationships grow. So far, BBBS has matched more than a million kids with mentors.

How do they know it works? Researchers have found that kids with Bigs are 46 percent less likely to use drugs.[11] And 65 percent of Littles say their Bigs have helped them attain higher levels of education than they'd thought was possible for themselves.[12]

That's not coincidence. Who we hang out with matters. Being matched with Bigs gives Littles an advantage, plain and simple. Bigs are contributing to Littles' lives, and every contribution to our lives has an effect.

MAX AND THE DOUGH BOY

Another inspiring BBBS relationship is the one between Steve McClatchy and Max Mitchell.

When a Big Brother showed up to meet one of the foster kids Max lived with in their group home, Max immediately wanted a Big, too. And so did the five other kids who didn't have one. To his credit, when the Big figured out that none of the kids in the house had parents, he tried taking them all out to play basketball or hang out. But he quickly realized he couldn't mentor all of them and suggested the others sign up with BBBS.

Thirteen-year-old Max ran to the program. "I wanted a mentor. I didn't trust anyone because of my past history of being abused, and I had no one to talk to and vent. I wanted to play basketball and have fun with someone."

Steve became that person.

"I'm the eleventh of twelve kids," Steve says. "I looked at my life and how many people I could turn to for advice. My dad was my hero, an inspiration for me. A lot of people don't have that. Going through life without a mentor, a coach, a guide, without someone to be there when you're about to make a pivotal decision—I couldn't imagine that. I didn't have a time frame in mind—just thought I'd help a kid with his homework, take him out to ice cream."

Steve and a BBBS staffer drove from his dorm at Catholic University of America to Max's group home in a gritty neighborhood of Washington, D.C. "We walked in the front door, and Max was so big— six-foot-two, 250 pounds—that we thought he was the house manager," Steve says. "He didn't speak—he mumbled at best. I was like, 'I'm here to see Max. I'm going to be his Big Brother,' and he nods. I said, 'Is he coming? Is he upstairs? Is he out for the day?' It took at least four rounds of asking where Max was for him to finally mumble, 'I'm Max.' I asked if he wanted to go across the street and shoot hoops and he was like 'Great.'"

From there they rappelled down mountains, played sports, watched movies, studied, hosted a radio show at Steve's college and worked together moving furniture on campus. Steve helped Max open his first bank account and budget his money, and he helped prepare him for college.

"He showed up to all my football games, showed up to the roughest neighborhoods in the city of D.C. Steve would show up," Max says.

"I was playing basketball at a packed high school. Steve and his friend walk into the gym, the only two white guys, and everyone else is like 'Who are these guys and why are they here?' That was Steve. He would come to every game no matter where I played at. He even reffed one of my games because we didn't have a ref at the school—he has done everything."

Meanwhile, Max's grades were suffering as a result of the learning challenges posed by his dyslexia. There came a point where the social workers, caseworkers, therapists and professionals who worked with Max wanted to send him to an alternative high school where he wouldn't get an actual diploma. Steve fought them on it.

"He can go to a regular school," he said.

"We don't think he's capable of that," Max's social worker said.

"I know he's capable of that."

"It's just not going to work."

"What if I guaranteed you that it will work?"

"You can't guarantee that."

"What if I guarantee it? I will be there every day studying if he has trouble. He will make it. I'm telling you—I will be there for him and get him all the way through high school without a problem."

"We're not sure."

"Let's do worst-case scenario—it doesn't work. We pull him out of regular high school and put him in the school you want him to go to. Instead of his first choice he gets his last choice. But for now, let's focus on his first choice: getting that high school diploma."

Seeing how dedicated Steve was, they gave Max a chance, and Steve stayed true to his word. He was always available to support Max in his studies. The evening before one big test, Steve called him.

"Do you want to study one more time?"

"No, I think I'm going to hang out with some friends," Max said.

"Come on, we should study one more time."

Max agreed and they studied in the basement of the group home for a couple of hours before Steve treated him to McDonald's. When they came back, there were police cars everywhere. There had been a random drive-by shooting, and two of Max's friends had been shot, one of them fatally—the same friends he'd wanted to hang out with that evening. If he'd been with them instead of studying, he would have been targeted as well.

Thanks to Steve's influence, Max also escaped the fate of high school dropouts. He went on to graduate high school and attend college for two years. Today, at age forty-six, in addition to working as a counselor to troubled youths, he's a confident and conscientious volunteer Pop Warner coach who shares his love of sports and serves as a father figure, role model and support system to kids who remind him of himself. He wanted to give back what Steve gave to him, and he's done it many times over, having coached two thousand kids in the D.C. area over the past twenty years. He gives every kid and parent his cell number, and they call him whenever they need to. He also meets with school principals to advocate for his players and make sure they're keeping up in class; he calls kids out if he sees them in the streets and knows they don't belong there; and he provides a great all-around example.

And he has some impressive stats to show for his hard work. Eighty-five percent of his players graduate high school, and 60 percent go to college—numbers that easily eclipse the average high school graduation and college attendance rates in these communities. As for what comes after, more than a dozen of Max's kids have made it to the pros—and they all come back to coach and cheer on his team.

Max credits Steve with the belief in himself that led to his success. "When he first met me, I would never talk to anybody. Wouldn't keep my head up. He would say get your head up, speak with confidence. I'd ask him to order for me and he made me order myself and worked on good posture with me. I had to go to prom and I was nervous, but he showed me how to dance. I got to experience so many different things with Steve—a whole other way of living. Steve is a blessing from God. Steve loves me no matter what. God knew I needed Steve."

He's especially grateful that Steve was willing to venture into a world that can be a dangerous place. "He embraced being in the 'hood. He was a part of my life and in the struggle with me. Once, Steve came over and ate ham hocks—ghetto food. It's horrible, and Steve sat there and ate it like it was the best thing going, and I'm looking at him like 'You don't like it.' He told me it was rough, and I said, 'I know, brother.' He was a part of my world."

In college, Steve had worked for Pillsbury, stocking shelves. When items were close to expiration, he was allowed to keep them and he'd bring the haul to Max's neighborhood.

"'Yo, your brother's here, your brother's here. The dough boy here,' people would say," Max recalls. "He'd pop the trunk and give out Pillsbury snacks to the entire neighborhood. People knew him and gave him high fives like he was one of us. Before the high school all-star football game, Steve gave me two Pillsbury stickers: Jolly Green Giant and Pillsbury guy. Then all the other kids wanted them, so Steve had everybody on my team wearing Pillsbury dough stickers on their helmets. The entire neighborhood loved Steve."

Steve's "'hood" was just as embracing of Max, but there was a learning curve for Max.

"He came to visit my family and he didn't speak," Steve says. "He was a deer in headlights. He walked into a house with twenty-five, thirty people and the weekend hadn't even started yet."

During his first few visits, Max had to sit next to Steve's mother, Kay, at dinner. At their house, if you didn't immediately eat the food on your plate, someone else ate it for you. She needed to provide Max some protection.

Initially, Max was also petrified of the 'burbs in general. For one thing, streetlights were few and far between. At least in the city he could see what was coming at him. Then there was the fact that Steve's family didn't lock the front door. With twelve siblings, you never knew who was coming or going or when. Max was so petrified that he slept in Steve's room instead of the room that had been made up for him. In the morning, Max—an early riser—wouldn't leave the room until Steve—a late sleeper—got up. He'd just sit and wait.

Until the morning that Kay came downstairs to find Max alone in the kitchen, having gotten over his fear.

"Can I have some cereal?" he asked.

"You can have all the cereal you want," she said.

After that, he was always the first one downstairs. "He'd eat twelve bowls of cereal," Kay says. "I thought, *He's no different than the rest of my kids.* It meant the world to me. I was so happy to see him at the table and for him to realize he was part of the family. We love him and he loves us. He's a gift from God, and I cherish it to this day."

Max now refers to Kay as "Mom" and has spent Christmases and every other holiday with the McClatchy family since he was a teenager. He's Uncle Max to Steve's college-age kids and often FaceTimes with them to check in and razz them about their favorite sports teams during big games.

Meanwhile, Steve still shows up for *Max's* big games. When his Pop Warner team makes the national championships, as it often does, Steve makes it a point to be there, even flying in on a day's notice when necessary. And he isn't about to settle for sitting in the stands with the rest of the fans. Even though fans are strictly forbidden from being on the sidelines during games, somehow Steve always finds a way. The players, who know him as Coach Max's brother, greet him with high fives, and he takes photos and leads cheers. Fittingly, the kids gave him a team jacket after a recent victory in Orlando. But even more fitting was the ring they presented, bestowing him with a title that's no exaggeration at all: "#1 Fan."

WHAT WE CAN DO

Many relationships begin with a single kind act. When my students need job-interview practice, I bring friends in for mock interviews. Often, a student will connect with one of my friends and a mentoring relationship is born. Or when a friend visits class to talk about her career, she might connect with a student. Then, like Tom and Steve, she builds time into her life for her new mentee, who—for the first time in some cases—has a mentor to call on.

In my family, mentoring is a group effort. My students are all wonderful young people, so I occasionally bring a few home for dinner, and luckily my wife loves having them over. This allows them to have a home-cooked meal, relax and meet a strong female role model.

When my students need work, my Uncle Steve usually has some tasks they can do around his factory. And better yet, he coaches them, too. A student might get paid for eight hours of work one day, and two of those hours were spent talking about life with Steve.

Steve has had a strong influence on my life as well. When I started my own company, he gave me discounted office space in his factory and coached me on hiring, firing and getting paid even though he had his hands full with running multiple small businesses that always needed more attention than he had to give them. When a company offered to buy my business, he came to New York with me to help with the process. When my business was sued, he asked if he could come to the trial every day and stare down the other side to make them nervous. Although I told him I didn't think that was a good idea, I love that he's the kind of guy to make that offer. He juggled more than most people, but when I needed something, he just added me to the mix. I remind myself of that every time someone needs help and I don't think I have time. Steve showed me I could make time.

Meanwhile, my cousin Jason is an expert in real estate, and he mentors both me and my mentees in how to find housing. To date, his advice has helped find life-changing housing for four of my students who had been homeless. And by the way, almost all of this group mentoring evolved naturally. My relatives would meet my students and see how impressive they were, and the next thing I knew they'd be asking how they could help.

Here are some practices that will help you to build great long-term relationships with people you'd like to mentor:

Show up

Max shared that Steve built a relationship with him by showing up. Whether it was a sporting event or a study session or a dinner of ham hocks, Steve was there for the little things, and that mattered. Who can you show up for this week?

Be enthusiastic

My grandfather was excited about anything I did just because I was doing it. To understand my business, he learned about blogging and online advertising *when he was in his eighties*. Just like he rose to the occasion, so can we.

Learn to give and take

I love when my mentors give me an opportunity to help *them* with something. You're there for your mentees. Let them be there for you, too.

. . . .

Your team, whether it's an athletic team, family, friends, colleagues or just a team of two—you and a mentor—has an indisputable influence on your life. The company we keep doesn't just say a lot about us— it's a major determinant of who we are. If you're interested in influencing a life, the coaching section of the *HumanKind* Hall of Fame (starting on page 217) lists more than a dozen organizations where sharing a little of your time goes a long way, from groups where you can donate an hour of your time to groups that will support you in building long-term relationships like Max and Steve's.

· ·

TAKE FIFTEEN MINUTES TO . . .

Show that you care. My Aunt Karen is seventy-five. She has four kids
and twelve grandkids in whose lives she's deeply engaged. She's also on
the boards of several nonprofits, travels extensively and seems to have
more social engagements than most people half her age. She's always
running and I'm not sure when she sleeps, but she still finds the time to
mentor many of her nieces and nephews. She talks to some of my cousins once a week and regularly has advice for me related to both work
and life. Once she called me because she'd read through every single
page of my blog (and that's a lot) and wanted to give me her thoughts
about it and about this book. When you make time for a mentee, especially when they don't ask, you remind them of their importance to you.
Even if I couldn't have used one bit of her advice, it would have been
an incredible gift. What can you do this week to demonstrate to someone how much you care? If you spend fifteen minutes thinking about
this, you'll come up with at least a few things.

· ·

CHAPTER

8

A NEW LENS
ON LIFE

"We can complain because rosebushes have thorns,
or rejoice because thorn bushes have roses."
—ATTRIBUTED TO ABRAHAM LINCOLN OR ALPHONSE KARR

Two shoe salespeople were sent to a remote area to open up
new markets. Three days after arriving, one salesperson called
the office and said, "I'm returning on the next flight. Can't sell
shoes here. Everybody goes barefoot." At the same time the other
salesperson sent an email to the factory, saying, "The prospects
are unlimited. Nobody wears shoes here!"
—UNKNOWN

WHEN JACK WAS FOUR, he loved to play superheroes, complete with
full costume. One day while he was portraying Spider-Man, dressed in
a bodysuit that even included "muscles," and I was Batman, wearing
a kid-size cape the size of a washcloth, we faced a dastardly situation,
as superheroes do.

"The bad guys are trying to take our dinner," I told Spider-Man.

"Don't worry, Daddy," Spider-Man said. "I know what to do." He ran to the kitchen, grabbed a spatula and started stirring the air with it.

"What are you doing?" I asked him.

"I'm making pancakes for them," he said. "If they're trying to take our dinner, they must be hungry."

I had it all wrong. I was thinking we'd capture the would-be thieves and lock them up. Good thing I didn't blurt out something that would have chipped away at Jack's generous spirit.

It's no secret that kids have much to teach us. Any parent certainly knows it. And when it comes to helping others, kids have a way of tackling problems head-on, without any of adults' cynicism or the obstacles we perceive.

Sometimes, that un*adult*erated perspective can truly change the world.

GABRIEL'S DAY OF KINDNESS

Before it became a day of light, it was the darkest day of Natasha Aljalian's life.

Natasha's three-year-old son, Gabriel, had been pale for months. When he also became fatigued, Natasha took him to his pediatrician, who told her that Gabriel probably had a virus. But Natasha suspected it was something else. When Gabriel seemed worse a week later, she made an appointment with a new pediatrician.

A few days before the appointment, Gabriel's preschool called. "He's not sick, but there *is* something wrong with him," the director said. Gabriel had lost more color and become extremely lethargic.

"I picked up Gabriel, and with one look I knew he had to be seen somewhere," Natasha says. "My husband had just left to go out of the country, so I immediately called the new pediatrician and said: 'You don't know me—we're coming in for our first visit next week—but something is wrong with our son. Is there any way you can see him today?' At this point it was late afternoon on a Friday.

They took him in and the new pediatrician sent him for blood work on Saturday morning."

After Gabriel's blood was drawn at Boston Children's Hospital, he and Natasha were on their way to a toy store as a reward for his bravery when her cell phone rang. It was the pediatrician.

"If you're driving, pull over," he said.

She did.

"We need more tests to confirm, but we're 99 percent sure Gabriel has leukemia," the doctor said. "Please come back to the hospital immediately."

"I entered a time warp," Natasha says. "It was just as it's often depicted in movies. The sun was still shining—but differently, not as brightly. The noise around me faded away. The world around me sounded like things do when you're swimming underwater. I heard some words, but I couldn't comprehend them. They were just random words."

Words like "hopefully . . . factors . . . are in his favor . . . long battle . . . many hospitalizations . . . three years . . . 70 to 90 percent chance . . . hopeful he'll live a long life . . . need you to return to the hospital right now . . ."

Breathe, Natasha reminded herself. *Breathe*.

In the back seat, Gabriel was clapping to the music in the car and laughing. When Natasha turned to look at him, he smiled and waved. "Hi, Mama!"

"That smile. His voice. It was as if it were happening in slow motion," Natasha says. She could feel her heart break at the thought of the fight that her son had no idea lay in front of him.

For the next two and a half years, Gabriel underwent chemotherapy and endured lengthy hospital stays. He was largely housebound to minimize his exposure to germs that might wreak havoc with his immune system, and Natasha spent almost every moment with him. She slept in his bed and soothed him when he couldn't sleep because of the effects of his meds. She persuaded him to undergo MRIs and countless other scans and tests. She rocked him and held him at the start of procedures. She comforted him when he was nauseated, anxious and scared. She begged him to drink and eat to avoid having to use a feeding tube. She took him to the ER dozens of times. She smiled at him, kissed him and hugged him to reassure him on the countless occasions when *she* wasn't sure he'd be okay.

But in the end, Gabriel made it through cancer-free, and his family's relief was matched only by their joy.

Gabriel still had to see doctors to make sure there hadn't been a recurrence, though, and on the night after a checkup, an idea came to him. He was in his bed with the lights dimmed. Natasha had just finished reading him a book and they were talking about the fact that the third anniversary of his diagnosis was coming up on November 3. As young as he'd been at the time of his diagnosis, now-six-year-old Gabriel clearly remembered parts of that day. He remembered that they were supposed to go to the toy store but went to the hospital instead and that he couldn't leave for a long time.

"It was a hard day for us. It was very sad," Natasha said to him. "But look at you now. You're strong and healthy. So we should be happy. But if you see me sad, it's okay. It will always be a hard day."

"Why can't it be a happy day?" Gabriel said.

"What do you mean?"

"We always feel good on secret Santa day. Why can't we do something to make everyone happy on my diagnosis day?"

My goodness, Natasha thought. *Coming from my child.*

Gabriel was referring to the family's secret Santa tradition, which had been inspired when someone left gifts on their front steps during the first Christmas that Gabriel was in treatment. He'd received a coloring book and some crayons, and his younger sister, Mary, had gotten a baby toy. There had also been a card, which the Aljalians kept on their refrigerator door and talked about all year. Eventually, they decided they'd like to serve as secret Santas for other people.

As the next Christmas approached, they thought of people who could use a boost. Then, with Grandma in the front seat and Gabriel in the back, Natasha drove to the homes of their designated recipients, where she and Gabriel would sneak to the door and drop off the package. It became a cherished holiday tradition, with Gabriel planning the days that the gifts would be delivered, the spots where they'd park the car out of sight and all the other details.

He enjoyed making others feel good so much that now he wanted to declare another annual day of giving: the anniversary of his diagnosis. "To turn a dark day into a light day," as he told his mom while lying in his bed. "Fill it with happy things."

"Sit up and explain your idea to me," Natasha said, and he went on to describe a day when all the members of their extended family would do good things for others.

Natasha got her camera, and as they discussed the idea, she shot a six-minute video that they could email to family members and close friends.

"November 3 is coming soon," Gabriel said in the video, sitting on the bed in his pajamas, "and you can do anything in the whole wide world to make it good. . . . And we are going to change a dark day to a light day."

After receiving the video, a friend asked Natasha to create a Facebook page for the video where people could later post about what they did on November 3. When Gabriel found out, he wanted to know how many people would participate. Natasha told him that they should try to get twenty people involved and that one of the joys of performing acts of kindness is keeping it secret, so some people might not even tell them about their good deeds.

That's not quite how things worked out. The video of a boy asking people to do nice things was posted in early October, and it was soon viewed tens of thousands of times. On November 3, reports of acts of kindness poured in from all over the world. Natasha's sister in Florida and a family friend in Wisconsin started things off, and before the end of the day almost every state was represented. Then the phenomenon spread to Armenia, France, the Czech Republic and on and on. All the while, map-loving Gabriel was in heaven, tracking the deeds across the globe with a smartphone app and marking the spots on maps that Natasha had printed for him.

Per the website's instructions, those performing the acts gave the recipients small cards explaining the idea behind "Gabriel's Day of Kindness" and encouraging them to consider performing their own acts of kindness. Many of the recipients emailed Natasha about their acts or posted responses on the Facebook page.

"I hadn't spoken to my mother in over two decades," one woman wrote. "Because of your day, I gave her a call. We reconciled and she saw her grandkids for the first time."

Another person wrote: "I lost my mother, my husband and then my sister just died. Someone handed me a rose with Gabriel's Day of Kindness mentioned, and I can't tell you . . . how much this one rose changed my whole day . . . . I was happy for the first time in a long time."

Some said they appreciated the acts of kindness so much that they were going to look for opportunities to perform their own every day.

As for Gabriel and his family, they were all over the place that day. They put flowers on the porches of homes—some of whose owners they knew, some they didn't. They went to a bus stop and handed out gift cards. They went to dinner and randomly paid for people's meals and watched what happened. Gabriel stood up a row of menus on the table in front of him and spied from between them as the waitresses delivered cards about his Day of Kindness along with customers' receipts, telling them their bills had been paid. To Gabriel's delight, the recipients kept paying it forward by paying for other customers' meals. When the Aljalian family left, the chain of kindness was still going.

The family also went to Children's Hospital and the Dana-Farber Cancer Institute to deliver toys, which brought back strong memories for Natasha. "When we went to Children's Hospital, I took a photo of him in front of Room 632, where he was wheeled in a few years before," she says. "So weak and little then and now strong and doing good. That was my moment. No matter what, that was my moment."

By the end of the day, the Aljalians had received Facebook posts and emails telling of 650 acts of kindness performed in fifty states and fifty-six countries.

"Is it still a dark day?" Gabriel asked Natasha that night.

"No," she said. "It was a great day."

"Can we do this tomorrow?"

"No. It was wonderful and thrilling, but it isn't something we could do every day." People had been stopping by that evening to share what they'd done, and Natasha was still processing the magnitude of it all.

"Can we do it next year?"

"Yes. Absolutely, if you want to."

The next year, Gabriel and his family began the day by giving out twenty dozen doughnuts, including deliveries to the local fire and police stations and a bank that had been especially supportive when Gabriel was sick. They gave out T-shirts, coats and mittens at a homeless shelter. They donated supplies to Cradles to Crayons, which provides children in low-income and homeless families with essential items, and sent cupcakes to various doctors and to kids getting cancer treatment. They also delivered toys to hospitals and gave gifts to Gabriel's MDs. And they again delivered flowers anonymously and paid it forward at the restaurant.

That year, 1,243 acts of kindness were reported on the Facebook page, with coverage in all fifty states again and in 105 countries this time. In the years since, both the number of acts and the number of countries have continued to grow.

"People are inherently kind and good," Natasha says. "Gabriel happened to be the catalyst for that. His idea just came at the right time, when people want to do nice things but, in the business of our lives, we just forget. This is a reminder that it's easy to do good for others. It doesn't matter if there is one act of kindness or a million. Each act is what's important."

In addition to the acts of kindness performed, at least seven people reported that they'd taken Gabriel's inspiration a step further: They started days of kindness to turn their own diagnosis anniversaries into happier days.

TURNING TRASH INTO TREASURE

Leave it to a six-year-old to show us how easy it is to shift our perspective. Sure, November 3 had been a day burdened with painful memories for Gabriel and Natasha, but if Gabriel could see past it to something entirely different, so could Natasha. If perspective can replace darkness with light, what *can't* it do? Like magic, it can turn a glass that's half empty into one that's half full. And it's well-known that perspective can turn one man's trash into treasure. That's what happened when Pamela Rainey Lawler built a charitable organization around the concept of filling a need with what others don't need anymore.

After reading *Starving in the Shadow of Plenty*, by Loretta Schwartz-Nobel, Pamela began noticing hunger where she hadn't before. The global starvation problem was well-known, but the book opened her eyes to the hunger plaguing America and her hometown of Philadelphia, where much of the book is set. The city was enjoying a restaurant renaissance and she loved dining out, but now that she'd learned of the vast number of people who were going hungry, she couldn't enjoy it anymore.

"The disparity between my life and the lives of those who couldn't escape the pain of not having enough to eat caused heartbreak that was too much," she says. "I knew too much to turn my back on this."

She didn't know too much about the restaurant and catering businesses, though, so she did her homework. She talked to industry insiders and representatives from food banks and soup kitchens about perishable foods that regularly went to waste, and she found out that there was both a surplus and a need but that they didn't always meet in the middle. A soup kitchen would arrange to make a pickup at a restaurant, for example, but due to the agency's limited resources, the pickup would fall through the cracks and the food would go to waste. What was needed was a middleman to handle logistics, and that was Pamela's opening.

But the industry professionals saw nothing but obstacles. Was it really possible to handle the food efficiently enough that it wouldn't spoil? If it did spoil, would it make people sick, and would the restaurants be held liable? Could food really get to a nearby nonprofit that was equipped to distribute it when no one had been able to make that work before? Luckily, Pamela's lack of experience in the industry prevented her from recognizing the scale of the potential obstacles, and she jumped in with both feet.

She raised $1,500 and left her marketing job to create a transportation link between food that would otherwise be discarded and a handful of groups that could get it to hungry people most efficiently. Once she had a list of the agencies' needs and storage capacity, she made connections with restaurants, caterers, grocers and farmers markets.

In the earliest days, when she would get a call from a restaurant telling her that excess food was available, she'd pick up the food herself in her Subaru station wagon and deliver it to the appropriate agency—often late at night, after the dinner rush or a party. If a delivery needed to be made during the day while her three children were home, they'd help her. A true grassroots operation.

As volunteers joined her effort, though, the business grew, and it wasn't long before the nonprofit she'd named Philabundance received a grant that allowed her to hire a driver, freeing up her time to focus on logistics, raising money for more vehicles and serving more people.

Among the people Philabundance has helped is Melanie Hudson, who fell on hard times after her husband of seventeen years died. Soon after, her employer lost a government contract, resulting in her layoff from the job she'd held for fifteen years. The Hudsons had suddenly gone from a two-income family to a no-income family.

She and teenage daughter Veronica moved into a small studio

apartment and cut all unnecessary expenses. Melanie became a full-time aide for a child with special needs, and Veronica got a part-time job. But even that wasn't enough to keep them above the poverty line. Every few months Melanie would get another letter saying that something else was getting shut off, and she'd have to figure out how to get it turned back on.

"An awful merry-go-round," as she describes it.

A gifted cook, Melanie had always loved to make dinner for friends and family, but now there was no room for guests and no food to cook. "Before we had financial problems, Mom cooked wonderful meals, especially this one stew with chicken, cabbage and potatoes," Veronica says. "And her macaroni and cheese is the best macaroni and cheese you'll ever taste in your life. But buying fresh food became unaffordable. We ate a lot of ramen because it was cheap, and we ate a lot of fast food."

And when there wasn't enough food, Melanie didn't eat, trying to fall asleep early to escape hunger pains.

Finally, she turned to the last resort: asking for help. For years, she'd noticed a line around her neighborhood church. She knew it had something to do with food, and now it was her turn to join the line. She felt like a failure. A college-educated woman with a career, she used to be someone who *provided* help.

"I was trying to play Superwoman and trying not to let Veronica see how bad things were. But when your belly hurts, you're not too good to ask for help."

So she got in the line, and just like that, fresh food made a return to their diets. And far from feeling like a failure, Melanie now talks about Philabundance from a position of empowerment.

"Philabundance gives me a chance to keep my head up and take a deep breath because I can feed my child. It gives me hope that this, too, shall pass."

Now, Melanie is determined to do what she can to provide hope to others. "When I have a little bit of extra money, around the time when Philabundance has a match program I will donate $25, so I feel like I'm making a difference."

Since its founding in 1984, Philabundance has grown to the point where it now supplies food to ninety thousand people a week in the Philadelphia area—all thanks to Pamela's ability to see that what some accepted as waste didn't need to go to waste at all.

FLOWER POWER

Across the country in Oregon, Heidi Berkman had a similar idea. During her years as a meeting and event planner, it always bothered her that so much money was spent on flowers that would be thrown away as soon as the event was over. Colorful, fragrant flowers in full bloom were simply tossed into dumpsters. Why not deliver the "used" flowers to people who need thoughtfulness more than just about anyone—people in hospice and their loved ones?

"I wanted to bring color, life and love to patients and their families when they need it most and when they least expect it," Heidi says. "End of life is such a difficult time for families, and they often feel isolated, alone and forgotten. A gift of flowers changes all that."

With the help of a few volunteers, Heidi started the Bloom Project in 2007 in her garage in the town of Bend, collecting leftover flowers and transforming them into new bouquets for hospice patients. As Heidi still had a consulting job, the crew worked mostly on weekends, and because they didn't have a refrigerator for storage, they'd pick up the flowers, arrange bouquets and deliver them to their hospice partners all in the same day.

Heidi says that when she started the project, hospice partners were realistic about what she should expect. "They told us it wasn't a given that this would work: 'Our nurses and social workers are going out into the field with medical equipment and computers and they have serious work to do and a time frame in which to do it, so for them to come out of their way to go to our administrative offices to grab flowers for patients—we don't really know how it will be embraced.'"

As it turned out, the idea couldn't have been embraced more enthusiastically. The administrator of one of the hospices seemed to speak for everyone when he called to give Heidi a rave review. "I can't believe how much this has improved the morale of our team," he said. "This one simple thing has made the nurses' and social workers' jobs so much more enjoyable. They're not just caring for dying patients but bringing them and their families joy through these special gifts."

Katie Hartley, former director of the home health and hospice organization Partners in Care, confirms the joy factor.

"The patients were just thrilled. Even the men," she says. "They would say, 'For me?' People cried, they were just so touched. It was a gift to them that someone would make a bouquet just for them."

The bouquets also bring a welcome change to conversations, like they did for Liz Taylor and her mother, Martha Hendrick, whose husband was in hospice.

"My mom and I were sitting in the room after many days of watching Dad's progression in hospice, and he's no longer very conscious, and we were talking about whatever we could talk about to keep as positive as we could," Liz says. "It's very difficult. It's hard to get your mind off the obvious in the room."

It was a rainy day, and when the nurse brought in a beautiful bouquet and put it on the table between them, everything shifted.

"The flowers led us to reflect on the kindness of others and from there to discuss the wonderful memories of Dad. We talked about how amazing it was that volunteers in our community who will never meet us, never see us, never know who we were, would be so thoughtful and put together such a beautiful, joyous and simple gesture to change the conversation in the room and celebrate Dad's life."

The flowers remained until Sandy Hendrick died four days later.

"I kept reflecting on the flowers, like if you have a wonderful memory from childhood that you think back on," Martha says. "I kept reflecting on that kind gift. It gave me an anchor. It gave me such hopefulness that life does go on. I breathed easier after that."

The timing was everything. "Instead of getting flowers at the end after Dad had passed, getting them when we were going through it and needed it the most was super powerful," Liz says. "Knowing someone cares, and seeing that kindness, is wonderful, and we still talk about that moment."

Liz and her mom were so moved by the gift that both became volunteers at the Bloom Project—a common occurrence. So many family members are so appreciative of the gesture that the project's volunteers now number two hundred. To date, those volunteers have helped the Bloom Project to deliver more than 260,000 bouquets to hospice patients throughout central Oregon and the Portland metro area.

CHANGING THE CONVERSATION

Heidi and Pamela saw their efforts result in the creation of sizable nonprofit organizations, but you don't need large forums like those to share your perspective. I once got a lesson in perspective in an entrepreneurship class I taught to teens. Although *I* was the teacher, it was another case of learning from someone much younger than me.

The class met two days a week at the Achieving Independence Center (AIC), a Philadelphia nonprofit that serves youths who are or have been in foster care beyond the age of fourteen. Having been through enormous trauma, our students were suffering because of circumstances beyond their control. They'd lived in as many as a dozen foster homes and been bounced among as many schools. Many had been abused and faced homelessness, and the system couldn't find most of them stable housing. Almost all of them were understandably angry.

After school, the students would come to the AIC to learn resilience and life skills that other kids typically learn from their parents. When they would arrive, the receptionist or one of the security guards would buzz them in—it was important to keep a close eye on things because the anger that was sometimes just beneath the surface could break through within seconds. Two students might exchange words, and fists would fly before the staff even had a chance to try to de-escalate the situation. That happened once in my own class during my early days of teaching there. On another day, a student threatened my co-teacher. Then there was the time a student from another class ran into my room, took the snacks I'd brought for my students and ran out with them. "You must be new," one of the security guards said to me afterward. "You need to close and lock your door when you're teaching."

Suffice it to say I had no idea what I was doing, but I knew I was in the right place. I left school after my failures all the more motivated to figure out how to teach a productive class and add something useful to these kids' lives.

The challenges didn't always involve student behavior, though. There was also a mind-set to overcome. At the start of each class, we'd take a few minutes to discuss what was happening in the students' lives, and they generally focused on what they were unhappy about. On a typical day, one might complain that she was on her fourth social worker due to turnover at Social Services, one might report that his foster parents weren't allowing him as much food as he wanted and several might talk about having to tell their stories yet again to new caseworkers—stories that were painful to relive. The students seemed to need to vent their feelings, but it wasn't the greatest way to motivate them to get on the phone or hit the streets to sell the products and services they'd created for our entrepreneurship class.

But one young woman didn't dwell on the negative. Instead, Yasmiyn always said something positive and pointed out her classmates' strengths. "Elijah, I love the progress you're making on your handyman business cards," she might say. Or, "Jasmine, I'm so impressed that your business is a nonprofit that will help other kids like us. You've got a huge heart." One day Yasmiyn noticed Thomas's expertise as a persuasive speaker and complimented him on his verbal skills. Another day, she said how impressed she was that Diamond already had T-shirts produced and was out trying to sell them when most of the class was still in the product development stage.

The other students would transform when Yasmiyn pointed out the positive. Rigid bodies would relax and smiles would spread around the room. Before long, Yasmiyn's classmates were joining in, offering supportive observations of their own. By taking the small step of expressing the good she saw, Yasmiyn brought about an immediate change in her peers and a long-term change in the tone of our class. She helped her classmates to see what was special about themselves and to recognize what was good in their lives. The result was that our class became a kind and supportive environment that the students truly enjoyed being a part of.

As for me, I take Yasmiyn's lesson with me everywhere I go. I look for the positive, and I almost always find it. And I don't keep it to myself.

BREAKING BARRIERS

Ryan Weimer shifted the perspective of others in a similar but very different way. He helped them to see what's typical about his kids.

"Usually, people are kind of standoffish with our kids," says Ryan, the father of two children born with spinal muscular atrophy. "You see a kid in a wheelchair and don't know what to say. This isn't because people are mean but because they don't know what to do. Wheelchairs can also be scary to kids who aren't in them."

Ryan and his wife, Lana, longed for other kids to see Keaton and Bryce without the barrier that the chair put between them. They wanted others to see the same things they saw when they looked at their kids: a couple of boys with great senses of humor and an abundance of imagination who love drawing, mastering video games and creating things. Then one autumn, Keaton planted a seed that would blossom in unexpected ways.

Keaton, then three, and Ryan were hanging out together when

Ryan asked what Keaton wanted to be for Halloween. "I want to be a pirate!" he said.

Ryan saw the problem immediately. "I looked at his chair and thought, *It will be hard for people to see what he is, all strapped into the wheelchair.*" But he also saw the solution: *I bet we can build a pirate ship around that.*

And they did. It took Ryan and Lana more than 175 hours to build it, and when Keaton saw the finished ship, his face lit up.

"Is that really mine?"

"Yeah. Yeah, bud, it is," Ryan said.

Keaton insisted on immediately trying on the costume, which attached to his wheelchair, and strapping on the fake parrot they'd made for him.

When trick-or-treat day arrived, Ryan says, "People had no problem coming up and talking to Keaton about his costume, and he became a superstar. As a father, you want your kids to have good experiences and feel included, and I saw that and it choked me up."

That's what sparked the idea to start Magic Wheelchair. "I didn't anticipate the emotions I'd have when I watched my son experience Halloween and watched other people interact with Keaton in a different way," Ryan says. "I saw people looking past his disability—the total opposite reaction than what we normally see, where there's that awkwardness around his disability. We'll go to the playground and our kids are in wheelchairs and the whole playground stops and just stares at them. We just want people to treat them like regular kids and see past their disability. With Keaton's costume, instantly he was included, and people and kids came right up to him. It was an amazing experience for him and for us as parents. I thought it would be awesome to do this for other families so they could have that experience, too."

Ryan started Magic Wheelchair in 2015 with a Kickstarter campaign that raised $25,000. In the first year, the project built eight costumes for kids in wheelchairs: two Mario karts, the Quinjet from the

TV show *Agents of S.H.I.E.L.D.*, SpongeBob SquarePants, the ice castle from *Frozen*, a Ninja Turtle van, a Pokémon and a Swan Princess. This year, Magic Wheelchair will build more than 130 costumes, and it plans to push the number higher every year. More than eighty volunteer teams across the United States build the costumes, each of which takes about two hundred hours of volunteer time. Typically, a team of three to five people builds a costume over three to four months. The build teams also help with fundraising, which gets the whole local community involved. Instead of just watching from the outside and saying, "That's great," community members have the opportunity to say, "I helped make that happen," Ryan says.

Besides Halloween, teams build costumes for Comic Cons, at which participants often dress up as their favorite heroes, as well as other events. The Make-A-Wish Foundation also reaches out to Magic Wheelchair for costumes, as it did when a four-year-old boy named Bryce (not Ryan's son) made it known that his last wish was for a special *Star Wars* party. For that occasion, a build team turned Bryce's wheelchair into a TIE fighter costume so he could be Darth Vader.

"He loved that TIE fighter and talked about it all the time and wanted to fly it around the neighborhood," Ryan says. "When he was in the hospital, he told his mom that when he was gone she should give the TIE fighter to another kid so he could enjoy it. His mom has memories of him for the last couple of months that are pretty precious memories that we feel grateful to have played a part in helping to create. Parents can carry those memories for the rest of their lives."

In the case of a young girl named Cassie, Magic Wheelchair made the difference between inclusion and exclusion. The build team turned her wheelchair into Green Arrow's motorcycle so she could cruise Comic Con as her favorite superhero. "Having this costume opened the door for me," she told Ryan. "I'm included and able to fully participate."

For Ryan, this is the magic that makes it all worthwhile. "Once the barrier is broken and you have a conversation with someone, you realize she's cool and not weird or scary because she has a chair. You see that she likes things you're interested in. The chair costumes break down barriers that scare kids off and create connections that last."

And the Weimers know exactly how precious these connections are for kids, which is why they try to spread the joy.

"I'm not a business guy—I was in nursing school when we first started making costumes—but I had to do this," Ryan says. "I love helping to build costumes that might change other children's lives the way the costumes helped my kids. When we find talent or something that brings joy into our life, we should strive to share it with others."

I CAN SEE CLEARLY NOW

Sometimes a shift in perspective doesn't just change the way we see something or someone, like a child in a wheelchair. Sometimes it changes the way we see *everything*. That's the experience Sanford Greenberg had when he was struck with his own disability.

In the summer of 1960, just before his junior year at Columbia University, Sanford's vision became cloudy during a pickup baseball game. The episode passed quickly, though, and afterward a doctor told him he'd had a bout of allergic conjunctivitis.

The episodes continued when he went back to school. He didn't tell anyone about them, but after a few months, he reached a point where he couldn't keep his problem a secret anymore. During a final exam, his vision became hopelessly blurred. Unable to continue his studies, he went home to Buffalo, where he was diagnosed with severely advanced glaucoma and referred to a Detroit surgeon.

A few days later, the surgeon took the only course of action that was possible by then: he destroyed Sandy's vision to save his eyes. At age nineteen, Sandy Greenberg descended into total darkness.

While recovering at home, he got an array of advice that was in line with the times. His mother suggested he work in his father's junk-yard. And a social worker confirmed that he shouldn't aspire to go back to school; instead, he could occupy himself at a work center that paid disabled people below minimum wage.

Miserable, Sandy was living in what he would later describe as a "horrific wilderness . . . in a frigid isolation, not wanting to see any-one."[13] His college roommate, Art, insisted on visiting, though, and he helped persuade Sandy to return to college, promising to read his textbooks to him.

Back at Columbia, Art did much more than that.

"My roommate helped me every day," Sandy says. "He walked me to class. He walked me back to my dorm room. He traveled around the city with me . . . . He bandaged my legs when I bumped into the concrete benches on campus."

Sandy also recalls one day when Art wasn't available to help him. Art had accompanied him to his appointment with a social worker as usual but, because of another commitment afterward, couldn't take him back to the dorms right away.

"But don't you understand I have a reader coming to see me at 4 p.m., and if I don't meet that reader, I won't be able to graduate with our class and it would be ruinous to my career," Sandy said.

They argued heatedly about it for twenty minutes and finally went their separate ways.

"It was rush hour, and so I inserted myself into the middle of [the] rush hour crowd, and they got me to Grand Central Station," Sandy says. "Before I knew it, walking with outstretched arms as though I were a sleepwalker, I ran into this large iron column, which cut my forehead open. . . . And the next thing I knew I bumped into some-thing soft—a woman's breast. . . . I fell over a stroller with a baby in it and the mother was screaming at me."

More than a few bumps and bruises later, he made it onto the subway and ultimately back to the university.

"As I walked toward the iron gates of Columbia, I bumped into a man who said, 'Oops, I'm sorry, sir,' with a sardonic *sir*," Sandy says. "Of course, it was my roommate, who had followed me the entire way . . . . I was enraged and I was going to hit him, but instead I hugged him."

It was a pivotal moment in Sandy's life.

"I had entered the subway with one particular vantage . . . and when I came out I had a different worldview. I had no more doubt and fear, and more than anything, I felt that there were no limits to what I could accomplish. That . . . episode defines me. It defined me then. It defines me [now]."

After graduation, Sandy attended Oxford University as a Marshall scholar, and it was there that he received a call from Art one day asking for $400 to help him get his music business off the ground. Sandy and his wife, Sue, had $404 in the bank.

"I found his request to be a gift for me," Sandy says, and he very happily sent the money to his old roommate.

As for Sandy, he went on to earn an MBA from Columbia and a PhD from Harvard; serve as a White House fellow during the Johnson administration; and help invent Variable Speech Control, a device that aids blind people by speeding up the playback of recorded speech. He and his wife have also established a $3 million reward for the most significant contribution to the curing of blindness. Inspired by John F. Kennedy's goal to put a man on the moon within a time line of 2,978 days, the Sandy and Susan Greenberg Prize to End Blindness by 2020 sets the same time line for its own goal. Three million dollars in gold bullion will go to "the person or group deemed most responsible for ending blindness by 2020."

According to the End Blindness by 2020 website, "The purpose behind the prize is to create a worldwide research community that will contribute its collective skills and resources *in concert*, step by step, phase by phase, to end blindness forever as a scourge to humanity."

If you doubt that it can be done, remember that no one thought we could get to the moon. And that Sandy Greenberg's social worker thought he should settle for factory work and minimum wage.

As for Art, he went on to enjoy an accomplished career as well and is one of Sandy's partners in putting up the reward for ending blindness.

And that $400 he needed for his music business? He invested it in a collaboration that came to be known as Simon & Garfunkel.

WHAT WE CAN DO

With Art Garfunkel's help, Sandy overcame his fears and saw that blindness isn't a barrier to achievement. Now he's contributing to the cause of helping the blind to achieve the *ultimate* shift in perspective. Gabriel asked, "Why can't it be a happy day?", and his Day of Kindness now inspires thousands of acts of kindness a year on his diagnosis anniversary. Yasmiyn decided to look for the good. Without her, my class would have been less successful.

It's all about perspective. Here are some ideas for changing yours:

"Believe the best rather than the worst"

This is one of my favorite pieces of advice. Jane Wells wrote it in 1886 in a poem offering marriage advice that's regularly cited online all these years later, maybe because the sentiment is still relevant and something we should strive for in all our relationships. Assume the best and remember that you're not a psychic. If you don't know what someone is thinking, ask.

Embrace intention

I've found it helpful to remind myself of other people's intentions. When I'm driving, I receive a steady flow of warnings from my wife such as

- "Watch out for that car."
- "You can't turn on red here"
- "You can't change lanes yet."

To hear her tell it, it's a miracle that the 85 percent of the time I drive without her in the car, I'm not involved in one accident after another. If you ask me, it's proof that I don't need the constant warnings. I used to get frustrated with the running commentary and sometimes made snappy comments. Then I realized I was taking her suggestions the wrong way—she's trying to be helpful. Heck, she's trying to save our lives. Many of the suggestions I receive (driving- and non-driving-related) are from people trying to help. Sometimes it's hard not to get annoyed, but I'm getting better at keeping it to myself. I remind myself of the person's intentions, and I know I'm lucky that someone cares enough to provide feedback.

Add yet to your vocabulary

Instead of "I haven't found a new job," say, "I haven't found a new job yet." The difference is subtle, but your brain notices.

Change "I have to" to "I get to"

My wife and I used to think some chores were a pain. We'd often say, "I have to do the laundry," or "I have to make lunches," or "I have to take out the trash." When Mia began chemo, she could no longer do those chores as regularly, being in the hospital or too weak much of the time. As she recovered, she regained her strength and she was ecstatic. "I'm so happy," she said. "I get to make lunch, I get to cook dinner and I get to do the laundry." Perspective.

See the positive

Studies show that when we see the positive more often, we're happier and we're kinder to ourselves and to those around us. We're also much more likely to see opportunities and solve problems creatively. Researchers have found, for example, that physicians, students, salespeople and toddlers perform better when they're more positive.[14]

Luckily for us, we're not locked into a way of viewing the world. We can choose to see things more positively. Here are some steps you can take to, among other things, teach yourself to look for the positive more often. Eventually, your brain gets into the habit of doing this and you won't need any prodding—you'll just do it naturally:

- **Compliment at least one person every day.** Maybe you begin the day by sending a short email or text telling someone why you appreciate them. "Just wanted to thank you for being a great friend." Or "I appreciated your call yesterday. Thanks for being so thoughtful." Besides reshaping how you see the world, you might make someone's day.

- **Keep a gratitude journal.** Every night, write three things you're grateful for. (By the way, researchers have also found that people who regularly write down what they're grateful for are 25 percent happier.)[15] You can also have a nightly family discussion about what happened that day that you're thankful for.

- **Perform a daily act of kindness.** When you perform a kind act every day, you'll start noticing other opportunities to be kind, creating a cycle of positivity in your mind. Think small—a thank-you note or letting someone cut in front of you in traffic. (Yet another way to make yourself and someone else happier.)[16]

- **Be mindful of who and what you expose yourself to.** Who you spend time with and what you watch, listen to and read all send messages to your brain that influence how you see the world.

Training your brain for positivity takes time, but it's a priceless opportunity to change your perspective and become a happier person. Before long, you'll see half-full glasses everywhere you look.

. . . .

TAKE FIFTEEN MINUTES TO . . .

Prove that you can train your mind to think differently:

Get a pen and paper. Take only three seconds to look around the room you're in, and remember everything you see that's red. Then take only a few seconds to write a list of everything you remember that's red, and don't read ahead until you've completed this step.

(You'd better not be reading this unless you're done with your list.)

Now write down everything you saw that was blue. Chances are, like most people, you don't remember the blue things nearly as well. You weren't looking for blue things. We see what we look for, and that's as much an asset as a shortcoming.[17]

. . . .

CHOOSE TO CELEBRATE

"Today, while I was driving my grandfather to his doctor's appointment, I complained about hitting 2 red lights in a row. My grandfather chuckled and said, 'You always complain about the red lights, but you never celebrate the green ones.'"
—FROM THE WEBSITE MAKES ME THINK

THE CAVERNOUS ROOM was filled with flashing lights that created a disco ball effect, the walls reverberated with bass-heavy pop music and all the kids were out on the floor shakin' what they had. No, it wasn't a nineties roller-skating party from my early teen years—it was the nightly "Dance for Your Meds" party at the Ronald McDonald Camp (RMC), where I was spending a week as a counselor.

Typically, taking cancer medicine isn't fun, especially if you're a kid. It usually doesn't taste good, and the side effects can make you feel nauseated. But at this camp, taking your meds *is* fun.

Why? Because the medical staff asked, "Why not?"

Celebrating is a choice, and sometimes asking "Why not?" is all it takes to create a celebration.

At RMC, the campers who take medicine at night don't just get their medication when they go to the wellness center. They also get a chance to blow off some steam before meds time and get some attention for their moves rather than their illness. It's a chance to own the dance floor and just be kids for an evening.

Granted, Ronald McDonald Camp is a place where creating celebratory experiences is part of the mission, but celebrations can also happen in places where you wouldn't expect fun to be on the agenda. Even in jail.

FIFTEEN

A few months before turning fifteen, Markeytia Poindexter was sentenced to Philadelphia's Youth Study Center—a fancy term for "juvenile jail"—for running away from a foster home where she'd been bullied. It was her third stint at the detention center for running away. She was outgoing and articulate, but she had a short temper, which led to frequent altercations and a reputation as one of the most difficult youths at the center—not a surprise, given her early childhood.

When Markeytia was three, her mother shot a relative outside their home and then locked herself inside, holding Markeytia hostage. When a police officer tried to enter the house, she shot him as well and then committed suicide in front of Markeytia. Afterward, because her father was serving a life sentence, Markeytia lived with her grandmother for two years until authorities removed her because of her grandmother's abuse. That began Markeytia's life of foster care, living in group homes and facilities.

By the time she was fourteen, she'd already served two terms at the Youth Study Center and, after running away from another foster home, had been living on her own for about a year, rotating between living with friends and living in abandoned houses and cars. She only occasionally attended school, missing months at a time, but when she did go, she excelled. The principal was so enthusiastic about Markeytia's journalism project on the Philadelphia mayoral campaign, for example, that she passed a copy along to mayoral candidate John Street. And Street was so impressed that he sent Markeytia a thank-you plaque after he became mayor.

One day soon after, the principal called Markeytia to her office. Markeytia figured the principal, impressed by her work and the plaque from Mayor Street, was going to encourage her to come to school more regularly.

"There's someone here to see you," she said when Markeytia walked in.

Markeytia's whole body tensed. She knew that the only people who would want to see her were her probation officer and her social worker. The principal had probably reported her poor attendance and alerted authorities that they could find her at school that day. She was in trouble.

As she and the principal walked down the stairs that led to the front of the school, Markeytia plotted her options for running away from another bad situation. When they got to the foyer and she saw the probation officer *and* the social worker waiting for her—along with a deputy—she bolted to the other exit. Another deputy was waiting for her there, though, and she was handcuffed and taken to court.

In the courtroom, Judge Kevin Dougherty—whom Markeytia had been in front of numerous times—was clearly upset as he read aloud the list of offenses from her file: going "AWOL" from her foster placement, sleeping in stolen cars, smoking marijuana. He seemed to become more and more upset as he read, and Markeytia didn't help matters by being flippant with him.

"These seem like very questionable choices," he said. "Are you all right, Miss Poindexter?"

"Not now that I'm standing here in front of you in handcuffs," she said.

In the end, the judge sentenced her to the Youth Study Center for the third time, but at least it was a familiar place by now. After having been in a dozen placements, she saw the value in something she could rely on. As it turned out, she was isolated in a unit by herself, and this stint at the center was much more peaceful than previous stays.

When her three-month term was almost up and she was scheduled to be released to a group home in Virginia—far from home so she would be less likely to run away—Director Richard Riddick came to her room. His visits to youths typically happened when they were in trouble.

"You need to come to the conference room," he said, his expression stern.

Here we go again, Markeytia thought. "I was good today. I didn't do anything. Why are you here? Where are we going?"

Mr. Riddick just looked at her and repeated himself. "You need to come to the conference room now."

The conference room was where youths usually met with their probation officers, social workers or family members. None of Markeytia's friends or family members had ever visited her at any of her placements, though, and it was past the hours when caseworkers visited, so she knew this couldn't be good. She walked quietly with Mr. Riddick and moved as slowly as possible. Anything to delay whatever awaited her.

When they got to the conference room, she hesitated.

"But, Mr. Riddick, I didn't do anything."

"Please just go into the room."

"But why am I getting in trouble?"

"Markeytia, please go in the room."

She reluctantly stepped inside, her body as tense as it had been the day she walked down the hall with the principal.

And then she saw the balloons.

What?

"Surprise!"

Mr. Riddick's wife and several staff members were also jammed into the small space for what was apparently a party to celebrate her fifteenth birthday. The room was hung with crepe streamers, and Mrs. Riddick had made fried chicken, potato salad and strawberry shortcake—Markeytia's favorite. "Happy Birthday Markeytia" was written in red icing.

In fifteen years, she'd never had a birthday party before. No one had celebrated her birth in *any* way, and she didn't know how to feel. When the tears started, she didn't fight them.

There were cards and gifts, too. "Mr. Riddick's wife gave me a Bible, and the staff members brought me braiding hair, which we weren't allowed to have in the center, and some CDs," Markeytia says fourteen years later. "The cards hung on my walls forever. I couldn't stop talking about the party or thinking about it. It was a high I was on for years."

Her unforgettable sendoff also brought her to an epiphany. Maybe she was worthy of love despite everything she'd been conditioned to think about herself. Maybe there were loving and understanding people in the world who cared enough to look beneath the surface and see her potential. Why else would *these* people have thrown a party honoring the fact that she'd been brought into the world?

"My guard had always been up, and I had trust issues because no one treated me well, understood me or listened to me. The way I had been expressing myself was the only way I knew how: to fight. I didn't know the words to say to tell anyone what was going on with me, so I was frustrated and I'd punch someone in the face. Then I had the director of the Youth Study Center arranging a birthday party for me, his wife, who didn't even work there, bringing cake, and staff who cared. I had to think about it. There *are* good people, and I had to be receptive to that."

The epiphany allowed her to finally begin to trust people and open up to adults and develop relationships. It allowed her to let people help her.

"I started thinking more positively. I was a little more open-minded and not as guarded. It felt great to trust myself to talk to people. I felt more comfortable about venting about stuff I held in, in the past. I wished I'd done that sooner."

The influence that Richard Riddick had on Markeytia is clear. In her next placement, she mentored other youths at the facility and served as a role model. As a result, when she was released a year and a half later, she was allowed to return to the Philadelphia area, where she got her first job, at a Taco Bell/Pizza Hut, and reported to the local high school to enroll. Because she'd had so many placements, though, no one could find complete records of her education and she was told she'd need extra years of schooling. So she got her GED through a nontraditional program instead.

She also took on a second job and continued her education. She earned an associate's degree in behavioral health and human services, followed by a bachelor's in social work and finally a master's in social work. Now she works with traumatized kids and their families, and her long-term goal is to open a group home to help girls and young mothers. She's also working toward becoming licensed as a clinical social worker so she can provide outpatient therapy and counseling to youths in placement.

"Without the birthday party, I would have either been in prison, dead or strung out," she says. "That's why I worked so hard to become a social worker. I want kids like me to have someone like me or like the staff that was supportive to me."

As a social worker, Markeytia has found herself in front of Judge Dougherty again, this time to advocate for children, and she's come to see the man who sentenced her and placed her so many times in a new light. When she reviewed her own case files, she learned that he'd worked behind the scenes to find appropriate placements and help resolve problems she raised with him in court. She didn't know that he'd taken what she said so seriously, investigating the challenges with her living situations that she'd expressed. Suddenly, she realized the depth of his passion for helping troubled youths like she'd been.

Now thirty-two, Markeytia owns her own home and loves living in one place with her four-year-old son, Zah'L. And she still has the Bible that Mrs. Riddick gave her.

"I keep it in my family room. When I see it, I'm reminded of the kindness that changed my life, and I think about how God has brought me very far and how I've been blessed. I've learned that your location is not your destination. Where you are right now should not determine who you are or what your goals are. You've got to keep going."

Richard Riddick chose to celebrate the fact that Markeytia Poindexter had been born. Finally, someone had chosen to recognize her potential rather than her case history.

Celebrating someone's life is an easy and obvious way to nurture someone's sense of self-worth. When you think about it, there probably isn't a more empowering gift you can give. If you've been fortunate enough to have birthday parties throughout your life, you may have no idea what power they hold. When someone throws you a birthday party, the message is that they're happy you're here—they value your existence. Imagine how you might feel about yourself if no one had ever gone to that effort. And imagine how you might feel when someone finally did.

MATH = FUN (!)

For those who still have doubts that there's room for celebrating in the bleakest of settings, let's look at something even bleaker than juvenile jail: math class *in* juvenile jail. My friend Dan Rhoton taught a mandatory math course at St. Gabriel's Hall, a juvenile detention center in Audubon, Pennsylvania, and students of his like Quamiir Trice can attest to the fact that even jailhouse math can be fun.

At age sixteen, Quamiir ended up at St. Gabe's as a result of doing what everyone around him who had money seemed to be doing: selling drugs.

"I felt hopeless at the time, knowing I was about to spend the next nine to twelve months of my life away from my family and I had no control over what was going to happen to me," says Quamiir, who had been living with his siblings at his grandmother's home at the time of his arrest. "I felt totally in the dark about my future."

But it was also a period of enlightenment. "I remember wanting to change the narrative of who I was. I knew I wanted to be a teenager again—I didn't want to be an adult. I felt like all my cousins and friends were living the life I wanted to live. When I was allowed a call home, I'd hear about how my cousin was on tour with his high school basketball team and imagine what it would be like if I was a regular teenager, not dealing drugs. I was determined to make something of myself."

The problem was, he didn't have a good history with learning. Before St. Gabe's, the majority of his school time had been spent flipping through textbooks and filling out worksheets—there wasn't a lot of actual teaching happening at his inner-city high school. "School was terrible for me. I couldn't stand it. A waste of time. A waste of energy. We didn't learn in our classes. I went because I looked young and couldn't get away with staying outside every day and selling drugs like I wanted to."

And he didn't have much hope that school would be a better experience at St. Gabe's. Who in their right mind would expect school in a detention center to be a positive experience?

Imagine his surprise when he discovered that not only was it better, but it could actually be enjoyable.

"Dan made learning fun," Quamiir says. "He turned our energy for competing against each other to math."

The highlight was a game called "trashketball" that incorporated a ball made of wadded-up paper and a trash can for the basket. When students answered an algebra problem correctly, they got to shoot the ball for points and prizes.

"You'd try so hard so you could shoot," Quamiir says. "The class with the most points at the end of the week got a prize, and the student with the most points got a prize. It got so competitive that people didn't want the prize. We just wanted to see our name on the board. Everyone talked about it at lunch—who had the most points."

"It's easy to make something fun," Dan says, "especially if it's fun for *you*. People do crazy things for fun. They run through mud piles, swim and bike for many miles or go in the woods and shoot at each other with painful paint pellets. They pay for this, and this doesn't sound like fun at all to me. The point is that what's fun is what you choose to have fun with. If I say, 'Sorry, we have to do this boring math and then we can do trashketball,' it won't be fun. If I say, 'Woo-hoo, you're not ready for this, but I'm going to blow your mind. I'm going to show you a video about the Mars Rover and it's on another planet and you can do the math that puts that there today, but you're not ready, so let's do some warm-up problems and play some trashketball and then we'll do this cool stuff,' it's fun."

When Dan began his teaching career, he had offers from two schools: St. Gabe's and the Julia Reynolds Masterman Laboratory and Demonstration School—considered the best magnet school in Philadelphia.

"I was trying to decide in May or June, so I went to both schools' graduations, and Masterman was great—kids going to Yale and Harvard, diverse and not everyone coming from wealth. Incredible school and inspiring. At St. Gabe's, these families are like, 'I thought our kid would be dead and they're *graduating*!' Masterman is great and I'd do a lot of great stuff, but I wouldn't make a difference there. The other place—they had drug dealers and these guys who did all this crazy stuff. That's where I thought I could do some fun stuff and have some impact."

Where others may have seen lost causes, Dan saw raw potential. "I knew by the fact that these guys shot at someone, stole a car, dealt drugs, that they were willing to take risks. And there would be a huge payoff if they put risk-willingness into areas that they were told weren't for them, like math and science."

During Quamiir's time at St. Gabe's, education became so important to him that he chose to stay a month longer than necessary so he could earn his high school diploma. As it turns out, St. Gabe's pushed Dan to greater heights, too.

"Students like Quamiir took away all my excuses for mediocrity.

When a young person comes through the door determined to dramatically change their life, it's hard to make excuses about how you had a bad weekend, don't like your supervisor, feel unmotivated today, don't have enough school supplies or need another cup of coffee. When someone is ready to change everything about themselves for the better, you really have to help them and get out of the way."

After leaving St. Gabe's, Quamiir was so eager for the opportunities offered by higher education that he earned an associate's degree from Community College of Philadelphia before moving on to Howard University, where he graduated with a degree in education. In 2018, he started his career as a teacher in Philadelphia.

"I'm hoping to give back as a middle school teacher, to use my energy and my experiences to help other people and guide them," he says. "I hope to inspire and motivate them and turn them in the right direction. Obviously, I can speak as someone who was going in the wrong direction, and I believe I can inspire kids to change just like Dan and others inspired me."

And thanks to his old math teacher, fun is sure to be part of his lesson plans—maybe even some trashketball. "Because it was so fun and that approach to math was something I never saw before, it made me realize anyone could like school if their math teacher approached math that way," Quamiir says. "And if you like school, there are many more opportunities open for you."

A HALLOWEEN FOR ONE

Extracting fun from difficult circumstances is like finding a port in a storm. And just like Dan provided that port for Quamiir, the neighbors of four-year-old Branden Witt were there for him when he needed them.

Branden couldn't wait for Halloween. He loved Lightning McQueen from the movie *Cars* and had a McQueen costume ready to go even though it was only September. He still needed a stoplight, though, because that's what McQueen uses to start his races, and he was beyond excited when his dad decided to dress up as one. But then Branden's doctor delivered some bad news: Branden, who was experiencing more than thirty episodes of sleep apnea every night and not getting spinal fluid to his brain, needed brain surgery. And it couldn't wait till after Halloween.

His parents, Carol and Bobby, knew how devastated he'd be to miss trick-or-treating, and they couldn't bring themselves to tell him. Instead, they came up with a way that he wouldn't have to miss it: they'd reschedule Halloween.

They distributed fliers to fifty-two families in their neighborhood letting them know about Branden's upcoming surgery and inviting them to participate in an early trick-or-treat night with him two weeks before Halloween. They didn't want anyone to feel bad if they couldn't take part, so instead of asking neighbors to RSVP, they provided each household with a felt pumpkin and a glow stick—those who wanted to take part could hang the lighted pumpkins on their mailboxes on the night of Branden's early Halloween to let him know he was welcome to knock on their door.

Carol and Bobby also invited family and friends to help by parking and waiting along the street to ensure that even if neighbors chose not to participate, there would be friendly faces to greet Branden and provide treats. For a change, Carol was able to make the rounds, too, instead of staying home to hand out candy, since this wasn't really Halloween.

As the band of trick-or-treaters headed out that night—eight family members and some close friends—the sidewalks were empty, but the neighborhood was far from dark: Glowing pumpkins hung from mailbox after mailbox, and the street was lined with friends, all waiting by their cars to hand out treats.

"We were floored," Carol says. "I couldn't contain myself with the joy I had."

So that Branden and company wouldn't be the only ones dressed up, some of the kids at the other houses were wearing costumes, too, and even the neighbors who usually had their lights turned off on

Halloween joined in the celebration for Branden. Every family found a way to participate.

The neighbors also gave Branden activity sets, Matchbox cars and other toys he could use during his stay in the hospital. In fact, he received so many gifts that by the time the Witts had visited all the houses, the wagon they'd brought to pull him in when he got tired had been filled and emptied three times.

"The amount of love that we were shown was just amazing," Carol says. "And Branden was so excited I don't think he even noticed that no other kids were trick-or-treating."

As for Branden's surgery, it went well, and he's a happy eight-year-old now. This year he went trick-or-treating on Halloween with the rest of the kids in the neighborhood and had a great time, but that Halloween of 2015 will always be the most special one for Carol and Bobby.

"Words of gratitude aren't enough for us to express the love our neighbors showed to our son and to us," Carol says. "It's nice to know that people come together in the time of need and to lift up a child facing huge events that are happening in his life."

SANTA: THE NEXT GENERATION

Branden's neighbors obviously appreciated the role that holidays play in children's lives, and their dedication to making sure he didn't miss one is an example of how powerful a simple gesture inspired by empathy can be. What kid wants to miss out on a holiday—*any* holiday? It's like not getting invited to a party.

And what about the holiday that so many kids suddenly miss out on after celebrating it their whole lives? The holiday whose icon they suddenly stop believing in? Is the loss of that particular holiday "magic" just a rite of passage that kids have to endure? The family of Millie Caldwell didn't think so, and they started a tradition aimed at both easing the transition for the children and cultivating an appreciation of the true meaning of Christmas.

It started during the Great Depression, when Millie and her

parents lived in the old family farmhouse in South Dakota with her grandparents and her uncles. Christmas was approaching, and Millie's grandfather pulled her aside for a talk.

"You've been growing, and you've gotten taller and your heart's gotten bigger," George Edward Stevenson said. "In fact, your heart has gotten so big that you're ready to be a Santa Claus."

Six-year-old Millie couldn't have been more confused. "What do you mean?"

"I'm sure you've noticed that there are a lot of different people dressed up as Santa out there," he said. "Some of your friends might have even told you that there's no such thing as Santa. That's because they aren't ready to become Santa. But you are."

She still didn't follow.

"What's the best thing about Santa?" Grandpa said.

"Getting cookies?" Millie said.

"What else?"

"Everyone likes Santa?"

"And?"

"He gets to make everyone happy."

"*Right.* He gets the great feeling of having done something for someone else. And now *you're* ready for your first job as Santa."

"What job?"

"You need to pick someone who you think could use a present. Something to show them they're loved and to make them happy."

Millie picked her grandmother, who loved flowers. She found a potted plant for her, and to go with it she printed "FROM SANTA" on a small piece of paper. Thus the family tradition of turning the children into Santas began. It was Millie's grandfather's way of shifting her attention away from receiving gifts during those lean times and toward a different kind of gift—his way of showing the children what they could share with others at a time when they were so poor and his way of cultivating appreciation for what they did have. It also softened the blow when Millie inevitably lost her belief in Santa Claus.

In the decades that have followed, the tradition has been handed down from generation to generation.

"It's a special way of transitioning the kids from receiving from Santa to *becoming* Santa," says Leslie Rush of El Paso, Texas, Millie's daughter-in-law. "This way, the Santa construct is not a lie that gets discovered but an unfolding series of good deeds and Christmas spirit. The perfect time is whenever you see your child beginning to suspect that there is no Santa."

When her own children started to suspect, Leslie would take them to a local coffee shop, order some treats and have a whispered conversation as if letting them in on a secret. In the case of her oldest son, Adam, he chose a family friend going through rough times for one of his first gifts.

"They had nothing to give their daughter, and Adam said, 'I want to give her my bike.' So my husband and Adam worked on the bike—polished up the chrome, painted fenders and put Armor All on the tires. Made it look gorgeous. Handgrips with streamers and a bow. They put it in the back of our truck and drove over there and left it on the back porch. The day after Christmas, we went over and Sabrina just grabbed Adam and said, 'Look what I got! Look what Santa got me!' And the look on Adam's face was great. The rule is, you can't tell, because this is unselfish giving. He was bursting and didn't tell."

Now a father, Adam let his son Tristan in on the secret a few years ago, and Tristan got his sister a huge stuffed dragon. So the ranks of Santa's little helpers continue to grow and continue to celebrate a different kind of holiday magic—one they make themselves.

HAPPY HANUMAS!

Holidays aren't just for kids. Adults can be pretty disappointed at missing out on the fun, too.

The year we couldn't visit Mia's family for Christmas, my family knew she'd be feeling down, so my parents and my brother's family visited before the holiday and we christened a new tradition: Hanumas.

Given the "mixed-belief" nature of our family, it's a celebration of both Hanukkah and Christmas, and it's coordinated around everyone's schedule.

Just like any respectable holiday, Hanumas has acquired various trappings over the years. Apparently, I wore the same orange fleece to Hanumas three years in a row, and after a year of ribbing from my family, I decided to contribute an orange fleece to our gag-gift exchange. My mom ended up being the lucky recipient and insisted I give her the receipt so she could return it for the $5 I'd paid (I refused). Needless to say, I gave *everyone* orange fleeces at the next year's Hanumas and enacted a new holiday dress code: Everyone had to wear at least one orange item. Initially, they did just that—just one item—but eventually my brother bought orange pants for all the guys, and the orange accessorizing extended to socks, wigs, jewelry and nail polish. Over the years, Mia, Jack and I have become the Imelda Marcoses of orange clothes. How could we *possibly* live with ourselves if we wore the same Hanumas outfit more than once? One year we dressed up as orange Jedi Knights with oversized orange lightsabers MacGyvered from pool noodles and Dollar Store flashlights. Another Hanumas, we were superheroes with matching orange capes, jumpsuits and Zorro masks. We even jumped on the ugly sweater craze for Hanumas 2015, decorating sweaters with cartoon images of our family, blinking lights and tinsel. Yep, that's Hanumas.

I'll never forget the time my parents arrived for Hanumas right after we moved into a new house. We hadn't met most of our neighbors yet, and I really can't imagine what their first impression was when they saw the whole family—covered in orange from head to toe—walking up and down the street carrying gifts from the car. And for some reason, my dad was leading us holding a dog bone the size of an arm—the Grand Poobah of Hanumas, I suppose. Come to think of it, maybe that's why we had such light foot traffic that Halloween.

In the ensuing years, we've sent out whimsical postcards to save the date and generally fleshed out the holiday tradition whenever opportunity presented itself. One year, Mom's dessert leaked all over my brother's pants, and Rob said it was because the dessert was too watery. Mom, however, said it was because he ruined it while holding it in the car. Whatever the truth, Rob—who can't cook, by the way—vowed that he'd make the Hanumas desserts from then on and that they'd be better than Mom's. He's been good to his word—in part. He always provides the desserts, but they taste every bit as bad as they look. God bless Dad, though, who always eats his entire portion and claims it's delicious.

Another year, a young relative's girlfriend brought orange toilet paper whose label read: "Don't get shot with your pants down! By using Blaze Orange toilet paper instead of standard white TP, you let other deer hunters know you're not Bambi's white flashing tail." We knew instantly that the girlfriend was a keeper, and the TP tradition lasted, too.

We also have a different contest every year. We once did an egg-drop competition out of third-floor windows, and we had an "Olympics" where the family was divided into different teams to compete in "feats of strength and intelligence." My favorite competition was a *Chopped*-style dessert challenge. It was kids versus adults, and we learned that it's dangerous to provide thirty-five ingredients—the kids chose to incorporate every one of them into the ten desserts they made to "give them more chances of winning." As a judge, I was sweating and nauseated as I tasted every . . . single . . . dessert. Of course, the kids won. (The judges couldn't very well *not* award it to the kids, now could they?) And given that the prize was a trip to Hersheypark, the winners were understandably over the moon.

The kids always love Hanumas, whether they get a trip to Hersheypark out of it or not. Our son and niece think it's so cool that they brought Mia and me to their classes to talk about it during their studies of family traditions. Naturally, I showed up in an orange tuxedo, and I'd bet that Jack and our niece received a little extra attention from the school psychologist after we left.

By now, our home has two closets packed with nothing but Hanumas gear, including orange holiday lights, decorations and tableware, a seven-foot orange tree (and the three-foot orange tree that was its predecessor) and stuffed monkeys sporting orange clothes and accessories. Every holiday needs a mascot, right? We also have a giant box with framed pictures of all of us in a crazy pose at each year's Hanumas. The photos are displayed all over the house during the holiday as our own tribute to Awkward Family Photos. And every year, in the spirit of extending holiday giving beyond the holidays, my parents have made a Hanumas donation to a different charity.

All this because we wanted to cheer Mia up one Christmas when she wouldn't be able to see her family. But then, when it's a matter of coming through for loved ones, it's hard to overdo it.

WHAT WE CAN DO

During my first year as a counselor at Ronald McDonald Camp, I arrived not knowing what to expect from the campers. How ill would they be? Would they be homesick? How were they emotionally?

When my co-counselors and I were setting up the cabin, I noticed that Jim had brought a leaf blower. Given that it was the middle of summer, I thought it was strange. Maybe he wanted to blow the dirt out of our cabin every day?

"Uh, what's the blower for?" I asked him.

"To wake the kids up."

Um . . . . "Did you say to wake up the kids?"

"Yeah, they love it."

He was right. The whole camp wakes up early every morning when it's usually still cold out to take a "polar bear swim," and almost no one wants to get out of bed for it. So we told our campers that if they didn't get out of bed, they'd get "leaf-blown," and the next thing we knew, *no one* wanted to get out of bed. Not because they were still feeling a little grumpy but because they wanted Jim to stick the nozzle under their covers for an in-bed windstorm. Suddenly, an experience that most campers dreaded (counselors, too) had become another camp high-light, and certainly one they'd always remember. When I got home and told Jack about it, he insisted I wake him up with a leaf blower, too.

My experiences at the Ronald McDonald Camp remind me that there are people going through rough times, like Markeytia, Branden and Quamiir did, who need to celebrate—and that as busy as life can be, we can help with that. We have the capacity to find fun regardless of the situation.

Here are some ideas to ensure you inject enough fun and celebration into your life and the lives of those around you:

Celebrate the everyday

Every year, we celebrate "Mia Appreciation Day," during which I present her with a card and sometimes a gift to thank her for the amazing things she does for our family on a daily basis. Honoring someone on a day other than Mother's Day or Father's Day or their birthday makes it clear that you value them in a way that goes beyond observing the standard celebrations. It can be as simple as writing a note of thanks.

Start a new holiday

Eat a Banana Split for Breakfast Day on July 1? Eat unfamiliar foods from around the world on March 3? A Slip 'N Slide extravaganza on August 15? Why not?

Celebrate to raise funds

Our friends Mark and Rachel think their kids have more than enough toys, so they told birthday party guests that instead of bringing gifts, they could donate to Philabundance to provide food for the hungry. The birthday party for their two girls raised enough money for nine hundred meals. And Facebook has created a button so you can ask people to make charitable donations for your birthday. That functionality has raised over $1 billion for charities. I'd love to celebrate the employee who came up with that.

Help a stranger to celebrate

Kristina from Orange County, California, shared an experience she had in Trader Joe's: "I was saying [to the cashier] how surprised I was at getting out of the grocery store spending only $40, and I mentioned it's just me and the kids. I thanked her and walked out. She ran outside with a bouquet of purple roses and asked, 'You're a single mom, right? . . . These are for you.' I couldn't thank her enough before she ran back to her shift."

There are a whole lot of people you don't know who would appreciate being recognized. If we keep our eyes open like the Trader Joe's cashier did, we'll find them. The *HumanKind* Hall of Fame (on page 222) also lists many opportunities to help others celebrate, from the $25 you can spend to provide a birthday party for a hospitalized or homeless child to care packages for foster youths who are in college.

Have fun even in tough times

Our cousin-in-law's parents, Jeff and Kathy, sent us a box of gag-gift wigs that included, among many others, glorious eighties-vintage mullets, "hair band" hair and bright, tall troll dos. At first we wondered if we should be offended—was something wrong with them?— but then we realized we needed to have some fun. We staged a fashion show for our son, and it was a nice way to introduce him to the idea that Mommy would lose her hair and wear wigs. (Of course, if you're planning to do this, make sure you're close enough with the recipient that you know they'd appreciate it.)

What can you do to inject some fun into the lives of others? And don't get hung up on practicality—that defeats the purpose. Practicality certainly wasn't on Kathy's and Jeff's minds or on our friend Jon's mind when he arranged the junk-food tasting when Mia craved artificial-cheese products during chemo.

. . . .

TAKE FIFTEEN MINUTES TO . . .

Celebrate. When is the last time you celebrated? Whether you're running a household, doing your job, juggling too many things, or anything else, it's easy to focus on everything that has to get done and forget to celebrate what's already been accomplished, what's getting accomplished on a regular basis, or the people we love. Remember to celebrate the big *and* the little things. What will you celebrate this week? Plan it now.

. . . .

10

CATCH A WAVE (OR START ONE)

There was an older couple who had a very loving relationship
and were admired by everyone around them. At one point an
observer said, "I hope in thirty years my marriage has as much
passion as yours." The man replied, "Don't hope. Decide."

—UNKNOWN

"Go for it. It's ok not to be an expert. Amateurs built
Google and Apple. Experts built and sailed the Titanic.
Who would you rather be?"

—FROM THE WEBSITE MAKES ME THINK

WHEN MY FRIEND Vince Schiavone was growing up in Villanova,
Pennsylvania, in the seventies, his mother would make an extra portion of food every night, store it in a covered foil container and give it
to an elderly person in need the next day.

"It was just part of our dinner routine," Vince says.

Rita Ungaro-Schiavone worked at the YWCA and regularly visited elderly shut-ins who weren't able to care for themselves and had

no friends or relatives to help them. When she realized that besides being lonely they had little food in the house, she decided to start making the extra servings and delivering them.

It didn't take long to see that her visits were having a positive effect on the recipients' health and all-around quality of life. It also didn't take long to understand that if she was visiting and feeding a different person every day, there were countless others who had the same needs. So she told her friends and fellow church members about what she was doing, and what had begun as a one-woman campaign of kindness blossomed into a small nonprofit organization that she named, simply and aptly, Aid for Friends, which operated out of her home.

Rita established a system where volunteer cooks would fill a metal TV-dinner tray supplied by Aid for Friends with the same food they made for their families each night and put the tray in the freezer. Then they'd bring a week's worth of meals to a partner church, synagogue or social organization, which would store the meals in a freezer Rita had donated.

When it was time to deliver them, volunteers would take the meals to the same recipients every week, and that's where the "Friends" part of the equation came in. This arrangement allowed for the kind of deep friendships that can only develop over time, like the one between Anne McGoldrick and Mary Brownell.

Mary was in her nineties and missed Heather Hunnicutt, the granddaughter she'd raised. "Grandma was my best friend and my wise soul," Heather says. "She taught me everything. When I moved from Philadelphia to North Carolina, we couldn't see each other as often, and it was hard being so far away from her, especially as she got older. After a while, she started telling me that it was depressing where she was living and that she didn't want to live there anymore. I kept trying to help, but from so far away I couldn't change her mind-set. She was so down."

And then Anne and Evan started visiting.

Aid for Friends had paired Mary with Anne, who often visited with infant nephew Evan. "By my third or fourth visit, we were just talking about everything," Anne says. "We just had a really natural friendship. She would be in her recliner and I would sit across from her and just talk about whatever."

And when Evan was in tow, he added a whole other dynamic. "Mary got tremendous joy out of being around Evan," Anne says. "She wanted to show him off to everyone in her building. She would be so proud and would call him 'her grandson.' Of course, the other women would say, 'Isn't he your *great*-grandson?' And she would say no."

Heather says Anne and Evan changed Mary's life. "Grandma loved that boy and would brag about him, and she considered Anne her daughter. Every conversation would be, 'Oh my gosh, you should see how cute he is. He's growing up so fast.' It was all about Evan or how sweet Anne was. It was the most amazing thing that could happen to her, and I'm sure that's why she lived until ninety-nine."

Mary died in 2016, and Anne finally met Heather at the funeral. "The way we embraced each other was like we were family and hadn't seen each other for years," Heather says. "We just couldn't let go. I just thanked her up and down."

Anne's impact on Mary had been so profound that it inspired Heather's mother to volunteer as a hospice companion. So Anne's model for providing comfort has resulted in comfort for numerous hospice patients Anne never even met.

And that swelling wave of kindness started in Rita Ungaro-Schiavone's kitchen more than forty years ago. She'd set out to help one person a day by making an extra portion for dinner, and her example inspired so many people that it turned into an organized campaign to provide food and companionship.

Today, Aid for Friends operates under the name Caring for Friends and works through more than two hundred churches, synagogues and community centers in the Philadelphia area to serve five hundred thousand meals a year. All told, more than a hundred thousand volunteers have served more than sixteen million free homemade meals over the years. Volunteers prepare the meals every day of the week and donate most of the ingredients themselves. Caring for Friends also provides recipients with items like smoke detectors and pill dispensers that make for a safer and healthier home environment. Thanks to all these efforts, many are able to maintain their independence and stay in their homes.

Rita died in 2017, but her legacy lives on in the hearts of the thousands of people her organization helps every year and the thousands of volunteers she's inspired, myself included. I joined Rita's movement through the Jewish Relief Agency (JRA), and a few times a year Jack and I make food deliveries to people in our community. Our few dozen deliveries don't make a statistical dent or even a ding in the vast number of people affected by hunger—one in eight in the United States and about 815 million worldwide—but hunger is solved one belly at a time. And what we do matters to the people we meet. When we delivered food to a man named Anthony in North Philadelphia, Jack also gave him a holiday card, and there were tears in Anthony's eyes when he said he would tape the card to the mirror in his room and keep it forever. Then there was Irina, who clearly had nothing but was so grateful that she insisted on rummaging through her house until she found a candy bar to give Jack.

We're one of the thousands of families who deliver food for the JRA, Caring for Friends and other organizations, and together we *are* putting a dent in our area's hunger problem. That's what movements are all about. You never know what's going to touch off a wave as we each play our part, but we just might set one in motion by simply following our hearts like Rita did.

"Mom made a difference in the lives of so many people," Vince says. "I learned so much from her—I learned the power of one person making a meal each day. I learned the power of teaching your children to make a difference. I can only hope to do a fraction of the good she's done in this world."

UNMAKING A MESS

Like Rita's, Tommy Kleyn's first step was small: taking thirty minutes to clean up a small area of a polluted riverbank in 2015. As someone who commuted to work on his bike every day, he was appalled by the litter strewn along the banks of the Schie waterway in Rotterdam, Netherlands. He wondered how he'd explain the mess to his soon-to-be-born son.

As he rattled off unacceptable answers to himself—"People put it there," "I never cleaned it up"—something clicked. Although he clearly couldn't clean up the whole five hundred–foot stretch himself, he could be the one to start.

It took him only thirty minutes to fill the first bag with trash, and it made almost no visible difference in the situation, but he made up his mind to fill a bag every day on his way to work. When he posted his progress on Facebook, friends soon began pitching in. With their help, only twenty-two days after the cleanup had begun, the litter was gone.

Now Tommy has another goal. "The idea is to motivate people to fill one garbage bag with litter each year," he says. "It only takes thirty minutes, and you'll be amazed about how good you feel afterward."

He's exceeded his expectations both locally and globally. In 2018 and 2019 he led mega-cleanups with hundreds of volunteers who removed twenty-three hundred pounds of plastic from a one-mile stretch along the Schie. In 2019, he also partnered with Lalo Negrete of Ríos Limpios, a cleanup initiative in Mexico, to create a global cleanup day, and they ended up with eight thousand people in thirty-four countries joining together and removing 197 tons of trash. On his Facebook page, Project Schone Schie, Tommy encourages others to commit to litter pickup and posts hundreds of photos and stories he's received from people he's inspired. The photos depict cleanup efforts with before-and-after shots, and the stories are from people in places as far-flung as Romania, Morocco, Algeria, Bolivia, South Korea, Hong Kong and the United States, all of them following in Tommy's footsteps. Among them is a post by Eddy Kong Thiam Huat and his friends, who were as appalled by the litter on "their" Malaysian beach as Tommy had been by the litter along the Schie. So they each started by picking up one bag of trash a day, and onlookers soon joined them and the beauty began to emerge again.

"After we started, we couldn't stop," Eddy says. "Seeing the results was awesome. We had never seen the beach that clean. That feeling of satisfaction is hard to describe."

And it's a feeling Tommy can pass along to his son, now that there isn't a mess to explain to him anymore.

GOODE DOING GOOD

By addressing a problem on a small scale, Tommy and Rita each inspired so many others that a movement took shape. But you don't need to identify a problem to start a movement. You can do it just by setting an example like the Reverend William Lemon and his wife, Muriel, did when they offered a hand to a young man who needed one.

W. Wilson Goode Sr. was fourteen when his father went to prison. Without him, the leased plot of land the family farmed was going to lie fallow, so Wilson's mother, Rozelar, relocated the family from rural North Carolina to Philadelphia, where Wilson's older sister was living and more job opportunities were available. Once they were settled there, Wilson noticed a man in a suit who walked past the family's house every evening, and one Sunday, Wilson asked him where he was going. The man said he was going to the Baptist Training Union, a Bible study group, and invited Wilson to come along. When Wilson accepted, little did he know the important role that the group's teacher and her husband would soon play in his life.

"I remember the first time I saw the city, having grown up in a sharecropping farm," Wilson says now. "All the big buildings and trains and trolleys were, frankly, frightening for me. And there were two people who helped me get adjusted to my neighborhood and school and helped me figure out what a teenager could do that was positive in an environment I was not accustomed to: Muriel Providence and her husband, Reverend William Lemon."

The couple were there for Wilson when he needed to talk, and they also pushed him at critical points in his young life. When he chose not to apply for college, for example, they didn't let it go at that.

Wilson had asked his guidance counselor for college applications as high school graduation approached, but he came away empty-handed.

"Don't even think about applying to college," his counselor had said. "Go find yourself a job in a factory."

So Wilson found a job in a factory.

But this wasn't acceptable to Muriel and her husband, Wilson says, despite the fact that no one else in their neighborhood had gone to college. "Muriel kept after me, saying, 'You don't belong in the factory. You belong in college. And we're going to send you to college.'"

At her insistence, Wilson applied to Morgan State University—and he was accepted.

"I was petrified, and once I was there, I still didn't have confidence," he says. "I could hear the words of my counselor that I don't belong in college. And I'm thinking that I'm going to go to this college and embarrass everyone."

Besides feeling that he was out of his element, every time Wilson came home, the Reverend Lemon's church took up a collection to pay for the expenses that his loan from the U.S. Department of Defense didn't cover. The pressure was on.

But he handled it. "After the first year, Muriel told me that I belonged there and to go back and show them what I could do. And I didn't do bad. And each year from that point on, with her encouragement, I became a better student, and by my last semester I was a straight-A student."

After graduation, Wilson served in the military, and when his tour was finished, he returned to his neighborhood determined to help kids reach their potential. He started an informal youth group where he encouraged and counseled young people, and he became involved in politics, which he saw as a bigger platform for helping children and Philadelphia as a whole. He went on to spend years serving in various political offices and eventually became the city's managing director and then its first African-American mayor.

After completing his second term as mayor, Goode continued to serve youths. When the White House Office of Faith-Based and Community Initiatives asked him to be an adviser for Amachi, a program that mentors prisoners' children, he thought about it a little and decided he wanted to do more than consult for the program—he offered to run it.

In his first sixty days as head of Amachi—a word that translates to "Who knows but what God has brought us through this child" in the Igbo language, spoken in Nigeria—Goode visited fifty pastors to try to enlist them to recruit mentors. Forty-two pastors signed on, and the first 450 mentors were soon recruited. Goode also visited prisons to meet with parents and tell them about the Amachi program, and many of them enrolled their children. Amachi was up and running.

Under Goode's leadership, the program has served more than three hundred thousand youths in nineteen years. As a former mayor, he's regularly offered lucrative consulting and speaking opportunities, but he's kept his focus on his life's mission of helping children.

In talking about the importance of mentoring, Goode mentions a visit to a penitentiary where he met a father, son and grandfather who were all incarcerated together. The father had even met his son for the first time in prison—a phenomenon that isn't uncommon. Seventy percent of prisoners' children wind up incarcerated themselves.

Goode finds this unacceptable, just as his mentors had found his factory career unacceptable. "We cannot and will not allow the errors of the past to dictate the possibilities of the future," he says, expressing a sentiment inspired by Muriel, in whose honor Goode named his daughter. It's because of that sentiment that at age eighty-one, he continues to run the Amachi program and work tirelessly to help youths avoid the fate of their imprisoned parents.

"Muriel Providence believing in me was the absolute turning point in my life, so I still feel a grateful obligation to young people to encourage as many as I can to do things and succeed."

RAISING YOUR HAND

Like Muriel and the Reverend Lemon, mentors often have no idea that their kind actions will spark a movement. But then there are those who have a movement in mind from the start. Seattle Judge David Soukup recognized a systemic problem affecting the kids in his courtroom and took a swing at fixing the system—a fix bound to benefit generations of kids.

"While sitting at juvenile court, I never got a night's sleep without waking up to wonder if at least one decision I made that day had been the best for a child," says Soukup, now retired.

When he would hear cases involving children, he was frustrated by the fact that he had to make difficult life-altering decisions on their behalf and yet there was no one tasked with providing a voice for the children. Should he send a three-year-old back to the only home she ever knew? Was her mother telling the truth that there had been no abuse? Or was he putting the child in danger?

The caseworkers and lawyers couldn't always provide the information Soukup needed, and no one represented only the children and spent enough time with them to tell the judge, from the children's standpoint, what was best for them.

I understand Soukup's frustration. In my time working with foster youths, I've seen how overburdened caseworkers can be and how they change jobs so frequently that they can't always get to know their child clients well or fully understand their needs. Likewise, lawyers representing the kids have extremely large caseloads. I've seen lawyers who don't even get briefed on a case until immediately before the hearing.

In 1977, Soukup came up with an answer: committed volunteers. He believed that with training, they could provide a voice for the children and assess their situations, ensuring that they wouldn't get lost in the overtaxed child welfare system or get stuck in inappropriate group or foster homes. As advocates and watchdogs, he believed, volunteers could offer a consistent perspective through regular updates and recommendations to the court. And he acted on that belief.

"I had my bailiff call six to eight people who might be able to find volunteers," he says. "We asked them to bring a brown-bag lunch to the courtroom to talk about training and recruiting volunteers to speak for kids who had been abused and neglected. A week later, there were fifty people in the room when I walked in. I thought, *This idea is going to work*."

At about the same time, Carmen Ray-Bettineski had just finished her master's in social work, and when she heard about Soukup's idea, she called him and asked how she could help. He asked her to write the proposal for his vision, which she did, and the proposal went on to receive Superior Court approval, allowing them to get started. When the initiative was announced, 110 people volunteered and Ray-Bettineski found herself in the role of the first executive director of a newly formed nonprofit: Court Appointed Special Advocates (CASA).

In the forty-two years since its inception, CASA has grown into a national organization with a network of almost a thousand programs and seventy-five thousand volunteers committed to protecting the rights of abused children in the foster care and child welfare systems. For many abused children, CASA is the channel to the one person in their lives who will be a consistent presence—and who isn't paid to be there. CASA provides an adult to explain to a child what's happening in court and work in the child's best interest, often navigating red tape and complex judicial systems. And research gathered by CASA shows that children with a CASA volunteer do better in school, spend an average of eight months less in foster care, and are less likely to be moved from house to house and more likely to be adopted than children who don't have an advocate.

"CASA is my lifesaver," says Ryan Dollinger, who came up through the CASA program and is now a social worker in southeast Texas. "I would have been lost in foster care. There are so many kids and not so many social workers. There were times that I didn't hear from my social worker for three or more months, but I always heard from CASA. I can never pay CASA back for everything they have done for me."

Judge Soukup wasn't satisfied with a system he believed could do better for our children, so he proposed to change it. Carmen Ray-Bettineski saw a need and asked how she could fill it. Soukup didn't advertise a position, and Ray-Bettineski didn't wait for a job to open up. Fortunately for the two million children CASA has served, these two game-changers didn't wait to be asked to fix the problem—they just raised their hands. After all, life doesn't always send out invitations.

A GIFT FROM THE ANGELS

Children in need is a common theme among the stories in this book. In the United States, close to thirteen million children live in households that don't have consistent access to enough food, 2.5 million experience homelessness in the course of a year and close to three million have parents who are incarcerated.[18] Kids have no power over these circumstances—they were simply born into unfair situations, and they're dependent on adults to address the problems. But often, the adults in their lives aren't able to come through for them, and their only chance is adults *outside* their lives, whether in the form of social welfare agencies or just individuals who care about these problems. Yes, the need can seem overwhelming, but remember the shortcomings of drop-in-the-bucket thinking. Small acts do have impact. With the exception of Judge Soukup, the people you've read about in this chapter weren't thinking about sparking a movement, and they weren't put off by a sense of hopelessness. They knew that offering hope even on the smallest of scales is invaluable. Fortunately, others knew this, too, and picked up the ball and ran with it. Sometimes that happens and sometimes it doesn't. The important thing is to do what we can.

In 1979, Salvation Army Majors Charles and Shirley White weren't thinking about helping thousands of kids across the country—they just wanted to help the kids in their own community who otherwise wouldn't get holiday gifts. It started at a shopping mall in Lynchburg, Virginia, where the Whites would listen to the kids' Christmas wishes, knowing how unlikely it was that they'd get those gifts. So they decided to put a Christmas tree in the mall and, after hearing a child's wish, write the wish and the child's name and age on a card that pictured an angel and hang it on the tree. The idea was that shoppers would take a card off the tree and buy the listed gift for that child. And it worked—the program served more than seven hundred kids that first year.

Three years later, the Whites were transferred to Tennessee, where they established another "Angel Tree" program. Then it was only a matter of time before publicity about it gained so much momentum that Angel Trees were sprouting across the country.

One of those programs, located in North Carolina, provided a fifteen-year-old boy named Jimmy with a gift that would prove to be a bright spot amid dark circumstances. Jimmy had been placed in foster care at the age of nine and grew up in group homes, foster homes and detention centers. He was homeless at times and lived a childhood marked by neglect and abuse. But the guitar he received through the Angel Tree program sparked a fire in him, and as long as he had it, no matter where he was bounced around to or what abuse he was enduring, he could turn to music for escape.

When Jimmy was sixteen, homeless and not attending school, he showed up in a shop owned by Russell and Bea Costner, an elderly couple. He asked if there was any work he could do for them, and they hired him to mow their lawn on a regular basis, which earned him enough to eat every week. As he writes in his memoir, *Walk to Beautiful*, Jimmy was taking a break from the mowing one day when Bea surprised him by asking where he lived. Though he replied that he lived up the road, Bea told him he was welcome to move into the spare bedroom. Jimmy figured they'd wind up kicking him out within a week just like so many others had done, but a week's worth of food and showers sounded pretty good and he accepted.

Just like that, Jimmy became part of the family. Russell took him for a haircut and bought him clothes for school, and Jimmy started attending school again. In fact, he never missed another day. He even turned out on Senior Skip Day and won an award for his three years of perfect attendance.

He also started going to church with the Costners, where he liked to listen to Bea play the piano for the congregation. Her passion encouraged him to pursue his own music, and when he joined a rock band, she was his most loyal fan. Whether it was at a pageant or a cookout, she never missed a performance, and she always sat in the first row.

Jimmy took voice lessons and practiced whenever he could. The first song he wrote—with Bea in mind—was called "My Only Friend." When he became a corrections officer after high school, he played it for the prisoners.

Eventually, he landed a job as a songwriter for a music label, and fifteen years after he'd met Bea and Russell, his first record came out and its first single went to No. 3 on *Billboard*'s country charts.

In the years since, Jimmy Wayne Barber—aka Jimmy Wayne—has gone on to release two more albums and six more Top 40 country hits. And he says his musical success wouldn't have happened without the Angel Tree program. The guitar he received ultimately took him down the path to becoming a musician, not to mention providing him with a platform for giving back.

"That's where it all started," he told *Rolling Stone* in 2014. "I would not be here, wouldn't have the success and have the home I live in, have the car I drive, the clothes I wear—none of this would have happened had it not been for a guitar. And where did I get the guitar? So I'm in debt and making sure that I do my part in raising awareness for a program that helped me out when I had nothing."

To do his part, he tells the Angel Tree story in a song and a novel, both titled *Paper Angels*. He hopes they inspire people to participate as gift-givers in the program.

He took a break from his music career in 2010 and used his stardom to help foster youths. Specifically, he walked 1,660 miles from Nashville to Phoenix to raise awareness about their plight.

Jimmy has also created a nonprofit organization, Project Meet Me Halfway, to help foster youths by inspiring people to become volunteers, raising money to support nonprofits that help abused and neglected children, and advocating for legislation to allow youths to remain in foster care until age twenty-one, which would provide them with more time to navigate the challenges of obtaining health care, education, employment and housing. (In many states, foster youths "age out" of the system at eighteen.) And capitalizing on his fame, Jimmy has recruited corporations to support Project Meet Me Halfway. Planning is also underway for the organization's first house for older foster youths. And in honor of the woman who made a home for *him*, Jimmy is calling it Bea's Home for Youth.

WHEN KINDNESS CATCHES FIRE

We all know necessity is the mother of invention, and when kids needed the comfort that comes from receiving gifts, Charles and Shirley White invented a way to fill the need. That's the amazing thing about need—when people hear about it, they rush in like firefighters to flames. Which is exactly how Liz Woodward's story started.

The diner where she waitressed was empty at 5:30 one morning except for the two firefighters from the Hainesport (New Jersey) Fire Department who were having breakfast and talking about a warehouse fire that had been raging for days. From their conversation, she could tell that one of them had just come from fighting the blaze.

"I had seen the news reports of the massive fire over the past couple days, so I could visualize where this man came from," says Liz, who was a student at Rowan College at Burlington County at the time. "I decided to pay their bill, and since I didn't have any other customers, I had time to write them a little thank-you note on the receipt before I left." Needing to get to class to turn in an assignment, she didn't get the chance to see the firefighters' reaction.

Afterward, one of the firefighters posted the receipt on Facebook, and when it went viral, people started posting comments asking what they could do for *Liz*. One of her customers suggested contributing to a fundraising campaign Liz had set up to help her father, who had suffered a brain aneurysm and been left a quadriplegic.

Specifically, she had started a GoFundMe page to give her dad the gift of mobility. The donations would be used to make his house fully accessible and to buy medical supplies and other items he needed in order to be comfortable at home as well as a customized van that would allow him to leave the house for doctor visits and to see family. Liz had raised about $30,000, but after the firefighters posted about her fundraising efforts, more than a thousand people she'd never met donated. Soon, she had over $80,000.

Meanwhile, Mobility Ventures, an Indiana-based manufacturer of mobility vehicles, heard the story and donated a van to the cause. Liz discovered that Mobility Ventures was also donating a van to a couple who needed a vehicle for transporting their disabled nineteen-year-old daughter. By law, though, Mobility Ventures couldn't pay the taxes on the family's van, and they were too high for the family to pay. So Liz used some of the money she'd raised to pay the taxes herself.

To date, Liz has heard from thousands of people in 134 countries who say that what happened that day in the diner inspired them to pay it forward in their own ways, from small acts of kindness to grander efforts of love and compassion. Some people paid for breakfast for police officers and firefighters, and others bought groceries for a stranger or paid a bridge toll for a driver behind them. One man stopped by a nursing home and visited a few people who didn't have family and hadn't had visitors in years. Others volunteered or offered their time, some donated to special causes and some just practiced being kinder human beings.

"I've received messages from people that included 'We are kids in Germany, and we started a pay-it-forward neighborhood' and 'Someone paid for our groceries this morning and he referenced your story, and I can't believe I found you,'" Liz says.

It's the ripple effect that giving sometimes has. "The story wasn't just inspiration but it encouraged people to act," she says. "That was one of the best parts. Even if it wasn't an extraordinary act that someone performed, just knowing that it changed their mind-set for that day—maybe they were just a little more grateful—makes me happy."

Liz herself is grateful to have a job that allows her to make a difference on a daily basis. "I love what I do. I serve food, but it's not what you earn that's important. Everyone has an opportunity to make a difference. Every table that comes in is a new opportunity to make someone smile, make them feel good, make them feel worthy."

WHAT WE CAN DO

The Reverend Lemon and Muriel Providence saw a child in need and offered him support. As a way of paying back their kindness, Wilson Goode went on to head the Amachi program, which has mentored more than three hundred thousand children who have incarcerated parents. Jackson Duncan was one of those children. He says his mentor changed his life and his perspective, leading him to start the Philadelphia nonprofit Focused Athletics, which helps inner-city kids use sports as a driver to attend college and succeed in life. "All of the kids who have been through my program and the thousands more we will serve owe it to my mentor," Jackson says.

When we help a single person, there's always the potential that many others will benefit. We all have the opportunity to affect the lives of others in a way that might bring about large-scale change. We can follow the example of practically every person in this book and start with one small action. The key, of course, is to choose *your* one small step and get started. Here are some tips to keep in mind as you chart your course:

Start small

Whatever your goal, the best strategy for averting the sense of overwhelm that can come with trying to tackle big societal problems is to start with manageable expectations of yourself. Like Tommy Kleyn and Rita Ungaro-Schiavone, choose a small enough action that it can be continued over time.

Start with one person

The Hall of Fame is filled with organizations that can help you take that first step. You can start as small as mailing a postcard, and you don't need to help everyone—just one person will do.

. . . .

TAKE FIFTEEN MINUTES TO . . .

Think about what solution you'd like to contribute to. What action will you perform that's small enough that it could become an ongoing commitment? Perform it now or add the date when you'll do it to your calendar.

. . . .

CLOSING NOTE

"You cannot get through a single day without having an impact on the world around you. What you do makes a difference, and you have to decide what kind of difference you want to make."
—JANE GOODALL

GROWING UP, I thought my town was just about perfect—loving homes, not much crime, no homelessness—and I wanted to do my part by helping others. So when I got to high school, I joined a mentoring group called Peer Leadership. I understood that many students were having trouble fending off peer pressure, and not being the clique type, I thought I might have something to offer. Little did I know that even some of my fellow counselors had bigger problems than peer pressure.

During a weekend retreat to allow us to get to know each other and prepare for our roles, I learned that several of the counselors—kids I knew—had experienced abuse at home or had parents with substance abuse problems and that the parents of another had kicked him out of the house. That was why they'd joined Peer Leadership—they wanted to help others like them.

When I got home, I dropped the bombshell on my mom.

"Did you know some kids in *our* town are abused and kicked out of their houses?"

Mom looked up from the newspaper she was reading at the kitchen table. "Yes, I did," she said matter-of-factly, as if I'd asked her if she'd heard it was supposed to rain that night.

Today, I recall that weekend as the time I discovered that not everyone is well-loved. I should have known. There had been signs. Even Mom had tried to give me a hint when she directed my brother and me to choose a volunteer project a year earlier.

"We're too lucky for you *not* to volunteer," she said.

I immediately thought of a buddy program I'd heard about at school for young kids who had lost parents or were experiencing other family trauma. I couldn't think of a greater loss than losing a parent, so that's the volunteer project I chose. Once a week, I'd hang out at the community center with my "buddies," who were five to seven years old, playing basketball, tag and kickball and generally trying to give them a break from their grief.

But those were cases of kids being cheated out of their parents' love by death. It wasn't till my time with Peer Leadership that I encountered the concept of parents' simply not loving their kids. How could that be?

From there, I started to notice *everything* that was wrong with the world: poverty, hunger, homelessness and a shortage of people doing something about it all. By the time I saw the news coverage of an earthquake that had struck Mexico City and killed thousands of people—many of them children—I was appalled enough that I decided to stop going to temple with my family.

That may not sound like a big deal, but until then I'd been one of only a handful of kids who sometimes led services at our orthodox synagogue (I'd learned Hebrew at Hebrew school). I was also the only member of my family who was gung ho about eating kosher. I didn't even have a problem with the idea of buying a second dishwasher so we wouldn't mix dairy and meat plates. All in—that was me. So it *was* a big deal when I made that break from temple.

"Not a good use of my time," I told my mom. "I'm sure a lot of them were religious people and they died in an earthquake for no good reason. I'm better off going out and doing good in the world."

I went on to use my time doing volunteer administrative work at the local hospital in addition to mentoring for Peer Leadership. In college I ran our school's equivalent of Big Brothers Big Sisters and joined the Youth at Risk program to mentor kids at risk of going to prison, and after graduation I spent a year as a tutor in a group home. Since then, helping others has been a passion, and it's something I've been fortunate enough to be able to spend more and more time doing.

There's no lack of opportunity for any of us to do good in the world. And there's no lack of incentive. When we improve others' lives, we raise the quality of life for the whole community. Kindness begets kindness. And whatever measures you decide to take, rest assured that they'll be deeply appreciated by at least one person.

Besides what you're doing for the world, you'll also be helping yourself in a very personal way. For one thing, helping others is good for your health. According to a variety of studies led by researchers at the University of Buffalo, Case Western Reserve University and the University of California, Riverside, doing good deeds makes us considerably happier and adds to our life span.

For another thing, you just might see good deeds coming back at you. Consider the stories you read about Liz Woodward and Sanford Greenberg and the story Candi Barry tells. When Candi was growing up, she'd spend two weeks every summer in the tiny town of Hope, Arkansas, where her great-grandparents owned a fruit and vegetable business. Her grandmother, Mamaw, would drop her off at Granny and Papa Pat's store in the morning, and she and Granny would play Monopoly while Papa Pat took care of stocking and counting.

"Papa Pat knew everyone who came into the store and greeted them by name," Candi says. "And he'd talk customers through everything and help them pick out what was ripe. Without the aid of a scale, he could shovel handfuls of pecans into a sack in the exact amount that a customer needed. That might not impress most, but it impressed the heck out of me. He'd tell me the weight and the price of everything they purchased, and I'd enter it in the big old-school register. Then he'd carry their purchases out for them. If he didn't know you when you came into the store, he knew you by the time you left."

Every Wednesday, Papa Pat closed the store and took produce to an area of town where many families lived at the bottom of the poverty scale. He himself had come from nothing, so he accepted whatever these families could afford to pay. "When they didn't have money, he accepted barter, good faith and a handshake," Candi says.

After Papa Pat died, Candi's great-grandmother moved into a nursing care facility. "All the nurses and staff members were wonderful," Candi says, "but I noticed that the care that one of the nurses gave Granny was particularly tender." One day when she was visiting, she made a point of thanking the nurse for her kindness.

"It's my honor to say thank you to *you*," the nurse said. "Your great-grandfather used to accept the crayon-drawn pictures of a little five-year-old girl as payment for those fruits and vegetables when her family had nothing." She smiled. "I was that little girl who drew those pictures. So, no—thank *you*."

....

We don't perform kind acts to be rewarded for them or to increase our life span—those are just possible side effects. We perform them because it's what we're here for. We were given the capacity for love for a reason, and the fact that loving acts tend to come full circle like they did for Candi Barry's great-grandmother seems to be confirmation that they're the right path. Loving acts help others through difficult times—can you think of anything that has greater value? Can you think of a better use of our time and talents?

Our acts of kindness, no matter how insignificant we think they are, can be life-changing for someone else. During Mia's treatment, every person who gave us the strength to push forward contributed to our entire family's making it through the experience unscathed.

It was Jack's teachers, Katie and Rachel, who were juggling an entire class of five-year-olds but still found time to send us pictures so we could see that he was having a great time at school. They also updated us whenever he talked about Mia's illness, and they took the time to understand exactly what we were telling Jack so they could answer his questions the same way we were.

It was the two dozen or so people who raised their hands to pick Jack up from school and take him to their homes on occasions when I wouldn't be able to make it. The woman at the school's front desk said it was the longest authorized pickup list she'd ever seen.

It was our friend Kevin, who, without my asking, set up a conference call with two expert nutritionists who explained to me what I could do to help Mia when chemo was crushing her appetite. He also offered to go to any of Jack's sports practices or games so I wouldn't feel bad missing them.

It was our friend Richard, who took me out for a beer when I simply needed a distraction.

It was the parent who sent us this note even though we didn't know her that well:

Hi Mia & Brad, what are Jack's plans for tomorrow? He's welcome to join us in the afternoon. And then we will be headed to my in-laws to celebrate Hanukkah out in Bala Cynwyd. We'd love to have him join us. Saturday Sophia has gymnastics at In Movement, then we are headed to the beach. Not sure if we'll stay a few days or the week. He's welcome to join us then also. (And we are only in Brigantine, just an hour away, so we can bring him back whenever or Brad you can come down and join us). We might stay and celebrate Christmas there, super low key. Just let me know for any or all. Lastly, I saw it posted that we can bring food when we visit. Mia, please let us know what you like and if you have any allergies. Thanks! Best KS

Each small act was a link in the chain mail that protected our family. I'm guessing those people don't know that it was only with each of their seemingly small contributions that the armor was complete.

Today, Mia is healthy and doing great, and thanks to the help of dozens of people who picked up the slack in every aspect of our lives, Jack is still the same kid who loves the Phillies, wants to make pancakes for bad guys breaking into our house and has a perspective we appreciate on a daily basis. Take this conversation he and Mia had during a snow day last winter:

"Let's come up with a plan for today," Mia said.

"I have one," Jack said. "To be awesome."

I love that plan and have made it my own. Why not think bigger than our daily routines and crossing items off our to-do lists? Each of us has the power to "be awesome" every day. If you say to yourself, "I'm going to make someone's world better today," it will happen. All it takes is looking for opportunity, following through and that resource we all have within us: love.

As you blaze your path of kindness, let me know what you find. I'll try to share your stories on my blog and through social media. Let's make good news travel as fast and as far as we can.

Brad
brad@bradaronson.com
www.bradaronson.com

PS: Thanks for reading my book and supporting Big Brothers Big Sisters, the nonprofit that receives all author royalties. If you enjoyed *HumanKind*, I'd love it if you'd go to www.bradaronson.com/review to leave a review. It only takes a few minutes and is a critical way to help other readers discover my book. I read and greatly appreciate every review!

THE *HUMANKIND* HALL OF FAME

There's no reason to reinvent the wheel. In addition to the organizations I've already written about, the nonprofits selected for the Hall of Fame make it easy to find the right ways for you to get engaged and change lives. You can choose from one-time opportunities like providing holiday gifts for kids in need to ongoing commitments like online mentoring of first-generation college students. Not every chapter has a corresponding Hall of Fame section, but I've noted the ones that do.

. . . .

Additional ideas and the most current web addresses can be found at www.bradaronson.com/book-resources.

Give Gifts

ANGEL TREE PROGRAM

The Salvation Army's Angel Tree program allows you to give holiday gifts to kids who might not otherwise receive any. You can use the site's zip code search to find the nearest Salvation Army location and see if it has an Angel Tree Program. Not every Salvation Army chapter has an easy-to-navigate website, so you might need to call your local office. If you work at a large company, some Salvation Army chapters will provide a Christmas tree for your business's lobby. The tree is decorated with paper angels on which local children have written gift requests that employees and departments can fulfill.
www.salvationarmyusa.org

COMFORT CASES

When Rob Scheer entered the foster care system, he walked into a house full of strangers carrying all his belongings in a tattered trash bag. Thirty-two years later, four foster children arrived on his own doorstep clutching garbage bags holding all *their* belongings. Rob couldn't believe that after thirty years, foster kids were still carrying their lives in trash bags. To remedy the situation, he founded Comfort Cases. The nonprofit supplies foster youths with duffel bags and backpacks containing a pair of pajamas, a blanket, a stuffed animal, a toiletry set, a book and a coloring book or journal. A $10 donation to Comfort Cases pays for one of the duffel bags. Donors can purchase backpacks and the items that are packed in them through the nonprofit's Amazon wish list. Needed items start at $6. (By the way, those four kids are now Rob's adopted kids.)
www.comfortcases.org

ONE SIMPLE WISH

Danielle Gletow started One Simple Wish after she and her husband became foster parents and realized that many children in foster care didn't have access to things other kids might take for granted, like birthday and holiday gifts, sneakers and school supplies. Donors can browse and fulfill wishes for these items. Wishes are compiled by social workers and other professionals who work with the children. One Simple Wish reached more than twenty thousand children last year. You can fulfill a wish through their website or Facebook page.
www.onesimplewish.org

OPERATION SANTA

The Postal Service's Operation Santa program started in 1912 when Postmaster General Frank Hitchcock authorized local postmasters to allow postal employees and citizens to respond to letters to Santa. Operation Santa, which operates across the US, provides the opportunity to give gifts to kids who write to Santa. You can browse letters online and choose a letter you'd like to answer with a gift. The post office does not evaluate the letters for worthiness.

www.uspsoperationsanta.com

SOLDIERS' ANGELS

Soldiers' Angels has multiple programs supporting military families. One program matches military and veteran families in need with people who want to "adopt" the families for the holidays and help provide them with a holiday celebration. Volunteers purchase a $35 to $50 gift for each child in a family and a $50 to $100 grocery gift card (depending on the size of the family) to help pay for a holiday dinner. Volunteers are required to donate $1 a month so that the organization can validate your contact information for the safety of our service members.

www.soldiersangels.org

TOYS FOR TOTS

In 1947, Diane Hendricks made a few handcrafted dolls and asked her husband, Marine Corps Reserve Major Bill Hendricks, to give them to an agency that supports children in need. When he reported back to her that he couldn't find such an organization, she told him to start one. That year, Major Hendricks and the Marines in his reserve unit collected and distributed five thousand toys. The commandant was impressed and directed all Marine Reserve sites to implement a Toys for Tots campaign, making it into a national program. To date, Toys for Tots has delivered more than 600 million Christmas toys to more than 270 million children.

You can bring new unwrapped gifts to your local Toys for Tots drop-off location. Typically, toys are collected from October through mid-December, but call your drop-off location in advance. Find more information and drop-off sites at www.toysfortots.org.

LOCAL HOSPITALS AND SHELTERS

You can contact local children's hospitals and homeless shelters for information about gift-giving opportunities.

Donate Money

Donations to the nonprofits below have an outsize impact and offer extraordinary opportunities to change lives. I've also listed a couple of organizations that provide research to help you find worthy nonprofits.

HIMALAYAN CATARACT PROJECT (HCP)

It costs a maximum of $195 to cure one person's blindness through the Himalayan Cataract Project (by my calculations[19]), and that figure accounts for all of the organization's overhead and other costs. At the time of my research, HCP also supported 534 training opportunities for local eye-care professionals so that HCP's work is sustainable, and it reached more than 1.7 million patients with screening and basic treatment. So for less than $200, you're curing one person's blindness, investing in basic eye care and training physicians who will cure thousands of people of blindness.
www.cureblindness.org

REACH OUT AND READ

Less than half of U.S. children living in poverty begin kindergarten with the skills they need to succeed. About 75 percent of them will never catch up and will be more likely to drop out of school than their peers. Experts say that the best way to help children learn these skills is to read with them and that birth through age five is a critical time for this.[20]

Reach Out and Read incorporates early literacy into U.S. pediatric medical practices to reach children in need. At each well-child visit, clinicians talk to parents about reading with their children and provide a brand-new developmentally and culturally appropriate book. The preschool language development of children in the program is three to six months ahead of their peers', giving them a better chance of succeeding in school. Depending on the region where you live, $15 to $20 provides the books and the program for one family for a year.
www.reachoutandread.org

MIRACLEFEET

One in every eight hundred children worldwide is born with clubfoot, a deformity that, if left untreated, leads to an inability to walk. More than two million children have untreated clubfoot, and there are about 175,000 new cases every year. In developed countries, clubfoot is often diagnosed via ultrasound and treated shortly after birth. Children who are treated early typically go on to live healthy, active lives. Unfortunately, 85 percent of children born with clubfoot in low- or middle-income countries have limited access to treatment. These children will often face neglect, physical and sexual abuse, a lack of access to education and the inability to lead a rewarding life. The average total cost for MiracleFeet to treat one child's clubfoot is $500 (including the organization's overhead costs).

www.miraclefeet.org

FISTULA FOUNDATION

Obstetric fistula is a childbirth injury that leaves women with permanent incontinence. Obstetric care has nearly eliminated fistula in developed countries, but there are more than one million women and girls in countries with limited health care access who do suffer from this injury. Many of them are abandoned by their husbands and ostracized by their communities. Fistula most often happens to women in their twenties and can be cured only with surgery.

The cost of a surgery through the Fistula Foundation is $586. On top of surgery, the foundation funds outreach to find the women who need treatment and provides social reintegration programs. It also trains surgeons and health center staff and provides resources, such as vehicles for transporting patients, that benefit all of a hospital's patients. Based on the total cost of operating the foundation and providing these services, I've estimated the cost to transform one woman's life at $1,053.

www.fistulafoundation.org

GIVEWELL

GiveWell is a respected authority in evaluating the most cost-effective giving opportunities. Used by foundations and donors, GiveWell looks for programs that have been studied rigorously and repeatedly, are transparent about their operations and are underfunded. Then it does extensive analysis to recommend the opportunities that it believes will have the biggest impact. Their recommendations are focused on serving the global poor because they believe that's how the most lives can be changed for the money spent.

Here are two programs that GiveWell recommends:

- **Helen Keller International's (HKI) Vitamin A Supplementation program in Africa:** This program reduces child mortality, saves and improves vision, and combats malnutrition by providing needed vitamin A supplements. HKI's program reaches millions of children in thirteen African countries. GiveWell estimates that $1.10 is the cost for HKI to deliver a Vitamin A supplement and that $3,000 to $5,000 donated to HKI will save a child's life.
www.hki.org

- **Malaria Consortium's Seasonal Malaria Chemoprevention (SMC) program:** This program provides preventive malaria drugs to children in Africa. GiveWell estimates $3,000 to $5,000 will save a life.
www.malariaconsortium.org

GiveWell's range for the cost per life saved reflects the variation in effectiveness across the countries in which each program operates. The numbers don't reflect the other benefits the charities provide with our donations. For example, HKI's vitamin A supplements not only reduce mortality but also help prevent blindness, anemia, and impaired growth and development of children, and the supplements minimize the severity of infections. The analysis also doesn't take into account the benefits of polio vaccinations, deworming and "mop-up" immunizations for kids who missed scheduled vaccinations that occur alongside the supplement distribution.
www.givewell.org

CENTER FOR HIGH IMPACT PHILANTHROPY

This University of Pennsylvania–based organization provides analysis on opportunities to make a social impact through philanthropy. Focusing on causes as diverse as disaster relief, major global public health issues and the U.S. achievement gap, the center translates the best available information into actionable guidance for those looking to make the greatest possible difference in the lives of others. Reports are available free at www.impact.upenn.edu.

. . . .

Note: As you evaluate nonprofits, it's worth digging into the numbers. For example, a mosquito net reduces the risk that a child will contract malaria, and a nonprofit might claim that if you donate $20, it buys a net and saves a life. But many of the children who receive nets would have survived without them, and many people won't even use the nets correctly.

It's also common for nonprofits to cite a cost per life saved (or changed) but exclude overhead and administrative expenses in their calculations when our donations need to cover those expenses as well. Ask if any expenses are excluded from calculations when you evaluate nonprofits. Along those lines, it's also common for nonprofits to report a "cost per surgery" that includes only the costs for the materials, leaving out labor expenses and the cost of running the nonprofit. In determining the cost per surgery for nonprofits, I divided the entire yearly expenses of the nonprofit by the number of surgeries; that's the literal cost per surgery. Of course, this leaves us with the highest possible cost of surgery, as some of these nonprofits are doing additional work, but I think it's the most accurate way to measure—and an indication of the enormous return you'll get on your donation if you choose to invest in any of these nonprofits.

Donate to Specific Individuals, Families or Classrooms

DONORS CHOOSE

When teacher Charles Best was photocopying *Little House on the Prairie* so everyone in his class could have a copy, he realized how useful it would be to have a way to connect donors with teachers and classrooms lacking resources. So he created Donors Choose, an online site that lists teacher requests for their classrooms and has fulfilled more than 1.9 million classroom requests. Donors can read through classroom requests and choose the school, class and project they want to help fund with donations as small as $1.
www.donorschoose.org

4 PAWS FOR ABILITY

This nonprofit provides service dogs to children in need. Because training service dogs is so expensive, a family needs to contribute $17,000 toward the cost of training a dog for their child, which is only a small portion of the total cost. You can help families raising money for their children's life-changing service dogs.

www.4pawsforability.org/dreams

KIVA

While working at a nonprofit in East Africa to help entrepreneurs, Jessica Jackley and Matt Flannery saw that the biggest entrepreneurial challenge was startup funding even though the required funding was often minimal. So they built a platform to fund developing-world entrepreneurs and in April 2005 funded seven loans for a total of $3,500. When all the loans were repaid, they realized they had a sustainable business. Kiva allows anyone to fund a developing-world entrepreneur. Ninety-six percent of loans are repaid, and investors are free to reinvest. Sustainable businesses are the result, leading to jobs and self-sufficiency—especially important to the 81 percent of borrowers who are women. To date, Kiva has provided $1.6 billion in loans. Your contribution can be as low as $25.

www.kiva.org

DAYMAKER

In 2014, a group of college students founded this platform to provide resources to children. Companies sign up with Daymaker, and their employees can purchase holiday gifts and back-to-school supplies from specific children's wish lists. The lists are compiled by Daymaker's nonprofit partners. Daymaker is also piloting opportunities for employees to engage with the children.

www.daymaker.com

FAMILY-TO-FAMILY

After Pam Koner read a newspaper article about the extreme poverty in Pembroke, Illinois, she contacted an outreach worker there with the simple idea of linking families who she knew had "more" with families who had less. She was given the names of seventeen of the neediest Pembroke families, and she persuaded sixteen friends and neighbors to join her in sending monthly boxes of food (along with letters) to one family each. From there, Family-to-Family has grown into a national nonprofit.

Through Family-to-Family, you can sponsor a family in need with a monthly box of groceries. You can sponsor refugee families, Holocaust survivors, veterans and working poor families. Partner nonprofits find the families in need, and Family-to-Family matches them with donors. These programs request monthly donations from $11 to $55. In some of the programs, you're able to connect with the family via letters.

Family-to-Family also enables you to send a book a month to a low-income elementary school classroom to supplement its library. Family-to-Family fills an important gap in communities where there's barely enough money to cover food, let alone books.

www.family-to-family.org

Bone Marrow, Organ and Blood Donations

BONE MARROW REGISTRIES

On any given day in the United States alone, the lives of 17,500 people with leukemia or other blood diseases depend on finding a donation of matching bone marrow or umbilical cord blood. Many of the patients are children, and according to the U.S. Department of Health and Human Services, only 30 percent will have a matching donor in their families.

All it takes to register to become a marrow donor is swabbing the inside of your cheek with a cotton ball and sending the swab to Gift of Life or another registry. If you're lucky enough to be a match, you'll be asked if you'd like to donate. If you choose to proceed, there are two ways to do it: marrow cells can be extracted from the hip bone, or blood from a donor's arm can be put in a machine where stem cells are separated from the blood and the blood is returned through the other arm. Side effects are usually limited to short-term hip soreness and the long-term euphoria of saving a life.

Gift of Life partners with registries in other countries, so patients can search globally to find their match. If you live in the United States or Canada, visit www.giftoflife.org for more information or to sign up to receive a cheek-swab kit in the mail. If you live elsewhere, you can use a list of global registries to help you become a bone marrow donor online: www.wmda.info. Research shows that younger donors provide the highest likelihood of transplant success, so Gift of Life donors must be under sixty, and the registry asks donors thirty-six and older to pay for their swab kit.

ORGAN DONOR REGISTRIES

When you die, your donated organs, eyes and tissue could save up to eight lives and benefit more than one hundred. There are currently more than one hundred thousand people on the U.S. organ transplant waiting list, and every day twenty of those people die. Unlike in many other countries where you're an organ donor unless you opt out, U.S. law requires that you sign up if you want to donate. You can become an organ donor via this five-minute online sign-up: www.organdonor.gov. You can also sign up to become an organ donor when you obtain your driver's license.

BLOOD, PLASMA AND PLATELET DONATION

You can easily donate blood, plasma and platelets. Due to blood shortages, donations are always needed. My wife received numerous donations of red blood cells and platelets during chemo treatment, and it amazed me that because of a lack of supply, the blood she received had been shipped to Pennsylvania from Michigan. The donation process is painless, and a typical blood donation takes an hour. Your blood can help up to three patients. www.redcross.org

Write Letters

GIRLS LOVE MAIL

After Gina Mulligan was diagnosed with breast cancer, she received more than two hundred letters of support—mostly from friends of friends. She was touched by the letters and started Girls Love Mail to provide that type of support to women recently diagnosed with breast cancer. The site is full of patient testimonials about the impact the letters make: "As I read them I started crying . . . I was so glad to see that someone . . . was thinking of me and wishing me well . . . It melts my heart to receive these letters."
www.girlslovemail.com

ANY REFUGEE

William Scannell IV started Any Refugee when he was nine years old after his father told him how people sent letters of support to "Any Soldier." Jesuit Refugee Services, which works in more than fifty countries, distributes the cards to refugee children. Schools use the act of writing to refugees and the educational materials on Any Refugee's website to teach about the plight of refugees and empower students to provide hope.
www.anyrefugee.org

CARDS FOR HOSPITALIZED KIDS (CFHK)

Jen Rubino's inspiration for founding CFHK was her own hospitalization as a child and teen. She sometimes felt forgotten, depressed, lonely and isolated. During one difficult hospital stay, she received a handmade card from a hospital volunteer that brightened her day. "When I got the card, I felt I was not forgotten and people were thinking of me. That is what I want to do for other kids." CFHK has delivered more than one hundred thousand cards. Justyna Griffin, activity and donations coordinator at Lurie Children's Hospital of Chicago, captures the importance of these cards to parents as well: "I think that the notion of a complete stranger taking the time to create something beautiful to convey an uplifting message to them and their sick child really touches them. Through their beauty, through simple words and wishes, the cards give parents a sense of optimism and maybe even hope. It's like they represent good energy of the universe that is being sent to their family in crisis. That matters and it helps."
www.cardsforhospitalizedkids.com

CARDZ FOR KIDZ!

This nonprofit delivers uplifting cards to kids in hospitals around the world. More than two hundred thousand cards have been delivered to kids in more than forty countries.

www.cardzforkidz.org

POST PALS

While hospitalized as a teenager, Vikki George found that receiving cards was the only thing that made her smile when she was bed-bound and isolated due to her illness. So she and other sick teens started Post Pals, through which anyone in the world can send cards or emails to hospitalized kids in the UK as well as their siblings, who often feel overlooked.

www.postpals.co.uk

MORE LOVE LETTERS

When Hannah Brencher was going through depression, she wrote encouraging letters and left them for strangers wherever she went in New York City. It was her way of paying back the love letters her mother consistently left for her. Then she wrote a blog post with the offer "If you need a love letter, just ask." Nearly four hundred handwritten letters later, the idea for More Love Letters was born. To date, the nonprofit has delivered more than 250,000 love letters to people in seventy-three countries. You can nominate people who you think could use love letters. The organization chooses new recipients each month, and site visitors choose which ones to write to. The letters are sent to the nominators, who read them to make sure they're appropriate before giving them to the recipients.

www.moreloveletters.com

LOVE FOR OUR ELDERS

Jacob Cramer founded Love for Our Elders after his grandfather died. Thirteen years old at the time, Jacob wanted to bring happiness to elderly people. According to the nonprofit, more than 90 percent of seniors living in nursing facilities report feeling lonely, isolated or depressed. Founded in 2013, Love for Our Elders distributes letters written in English to seniors in eleven countries.

www.loveforourelders.org

LETTERS AGAINST DEPRESSION

Robert Mason, a former 911 operator, founded Letters Against Depression as a response to the high volume of depression-related calls that came in. The organization sends encouraging letters to people suffering from depression, anxiety and other mental illnesses to let them know they're not alone. Recipients sign themselves up to get letters. Volunteer writers send the letters to the organization, which forwards them to recipients around the world. www.lettersagainst.org

COLOR A SMILE

Jerry Harris and wife Susanne started Color a Smile after Jerry was at a friend's house and noticed the colorful artwork hanging on the refrigerator. Jerry knew he'd soon have his own artwork from his then-infant son and wanted to share that joy with people who might feel forgotten. You can print a page from the Color a Smile website, color it and send it to Color a Smile for distribution. The site has "free art" pages if you want to create your own art to color. If you or someone you know could benefit from cheerful pictures, you can sign up via the website. Color a Smile has given out more than a million cheerful pictures to senior citizens, troops overseas, veterans homes and anyone in need of a smile. www.colorasmile.org

ONE SIMPLE WISH

Volunteers can send messages of love and hope to children in foster care. One Simple Wish will forward your letters to let kids know that they're important and that someone is thinking of them. Email info@onesimplewish.org for information.

Some service members receive no mail, and the websites of nonprofits that send letters to service members are filled with notes of appreciation like this one on the Soldiers' Angels site: "I want to start out by telling you **what a great feeling it is to open a letter from someone you have never met before and feel so loved by a complete stranger** . . . Thank you for all that you do." The following organizations coordinate sending letters and care packages to service members:

SOLDIERS' ANGELS

While deployed in Iraq, Patti Patton-Bader's son told her that he was one of the few service members receiving care packages, so she gathered some friends and neighbors and they began sending packages to his whole platoon. More and more requests came from service members, combat hospitals and families of service members, so Patti and her friends built an organization to match deployed service members and their needs with people who wanted to help. Soldiers' Angels sends letters and care packages to combat-deployed U.S. service members and cards to veterans and their families. The minimum commitment is to send one letter a month. Requirements for care packages vary. Volunteers are required to donate $1 a month to allow the organization to validate volunteer information for the safety of our service members.
www.soldiersangels.org

OPERATION GRATITUDE

While volunteering at the Los Angeles Airport military lounge in the wake of 9/11, Carolyn Blashek talked with a soldier who felt like he had no one, and she decided that every soldier should hear from people at home. So she founded Operation Gratitude, which sends care packages accompanied by handwritten letters and handmade items to troops, veterans, first responders, new recruits, and wounded heroes and their caregivers. You can choose which group you'd like your letters or handmade items to go to. So far, Operation Gratitude has sent more than 3.2 million care packages.
www.operationgratitude.com

ANY SOLDIER

While Brian Horn was serving in Iraq, his parents sent him an average of six care packages a week. When he called home to ask for more, they thought he was kidding. He wasn't—he wanted to give care packages to soldiers who received little or no mail. So Brian's parents started the Any Soldier website, which has served more than two million troops. Troops serving overseas request items that their units could use, from underwear and socks to baseballs and puzzles. You choose a request to fill, and when your package arrives, the person who made the request gives your letters or care package to people in the unit who don't get much or any mail. Keep in mind that this isn't as simple as bringing a care package to the post office. You'll need to download and fill out customs forms. The forms indicate shipping limitations you'll want to know before buying care package items.

www.anysoldier.com

One-Time Coaching and Mentoring Opportunities

DREAMWAKERS

DreamWakers connects classrooms to career role models by way of video chat because "students can't be what they can't see." Eighty-eight percent of students who have participated had never met someone in the respective speakers' professions. Working with fourth- through twelfth-grade classrooms, DreamWakers serves U.S. schools in which at least 50 percent of the student body is eligible for free or reduced-price lunch. Speaking of which, you can be a guest speaker during *your* lunch. Founders Monica Gray Logothetis and Annie Medaglia loved volunteering in classrooms when they were in college, but they didn't have the same flexibility when they started working. When they noticed that their peers had the same problem, they created this way to volunteer during lunch to bring much-needed resources and role models to schools.

www.dreamwakers.org

VETERATI

The transition from military to civilian life can be frustrating. After growing within the military and having significant responsibility, veterans are faced with the need to start over when they get out. Specifically, they have to figure out how to find opportunities and present themselves within the civilian system, which their peers have already been doing for years. To facilitate the process, Veterati offers volunteers a chance to provide veterans with valuable career mentoring. Mentors sign up online (it takes a couple of minutes) and note areas of expertise and a specific time and date to mentor (a minimum of an hour). Veterans, active military and spouses browse through mentors and schedule a coaching session through the Veterati platform, and Veterati connects the call.

www.veterati.com

AMERICAN CORPORATE PARTNERS

American Corporate Partners' AdvisorNet is an online forum where veterans and spouses of active-duty military can seek career advice for civilian jobs. Spouses are included because they often move every few years to support their partners and therefore don't have a strong network to rely on. Questions range from how to improve a résumé to the best way to get in the door for an IT job to how to negotiate a pay raise. Tens of thousands of veterans post questions on the forum, and after registering as an adviser, you can search through questions and provide suggestions in your area of expertise. Veterans can also search adviser profiles to find those who have experience in areas where they need help. American Corporate Partners says there's a growing need to help transitioning veterans given the Department of Defense's projection that starting in 2019 one million additional troops will be transitioning over the following five years.

www.acp-usa.org

SKYPE A SCIENTIST

Sarah McAnulty began Skype a Scientist when she was a graduate student at the University of Connecticut because of her concern that the political divisiveness in the United States was leading to a mistrust of science. Skype a Scientist pairs volunteer scientists with classrooms to make science accessible and fun through personal connections. The nonprofit also focuses on helping students see the diversity in science.

One scientist volunteer fondly recalled the time when she was Skyping with a class and the teacher reminded students that coding isn't just for boys. "It's true," the volunteer said. "I code every day, and I'm a girl!" Two of the girls in the back of the room threw up their hands and jumped out of their seats with huge smiles.

More than fourteen thousand scientists from seventy-five countries have participated in the program, along with more than thirty-five thousand student groups. Volunteers sign up for thirty to sixty-minute Q&A sessions.

www.skypeascientist.com

WORKFORCE DEVELOPMENT

Most workforce development programs are looking for volunteers to help with mock interviews, career advice and résumé help and can be found online. For example, in my area I'd search for "Philadelphia workforce development nonprofit." You can also find mentoring organizations through specific searches like "mentoring women in Philadelphia."

Long-Term Mentoring and Coaching Opportunities

MENTOR: THE NATIONAL MENTORING PARTNERSHIP

This national organization has a database of opportunities for mentoring people twenty-four and younger, searchable by zip code. You can filter by geography, age of people you'd like to mentor, type of mentoring and how you'd like to provide mentoring (online, one-on-one, group). Filters also include young people who are pregnant, homeless, academically gifted, struggling parents and first-generation college students.

www.mentoring.org

BIG BROTHERS BIG SISTERS (BBBS)

BBBS was founded in 1904 when Ernest Coulter, a New York City court clerk, saw more and more children coming through his courtroom and recognized that caring adults could help many of these kids stay out of trouble. Since then, BBBS has grown across the United States and facilitates more than a hundred thousand mentoring relationships every year. As a mentor you'll spend a few hours twice a month with a child. The goal is to create lifelong friendships, but you're committing only for a year.

www.bbbs.org

COURT APPOINTED SPECIAL ADVOCATES (CASA)

CASA supports children who are going through the judicial system because they've experienced neglect or abuse. Advocates are paired with children whom they get to know, and they help judges and others to understand what the children need in order to find safe permanent homes. As a volunteer,

you'll complete thirty hours of training and then you'll be matched with a child and be expected to volunteer for the length of their case. A case generally lasts a year and a half and requires about five to ten hours a month. Research has shown that children paired with a CASA volunteer have a much higher likelihood of finding a safe permanent home, do better in school and are less likely to be bounced from home to home.
www.casaforchildren.org

EXPERIENCE CORPS

This AARP program matches adults fifty and older with students in kindergarten through third grade who are struggling to read. You're expected to complete twenty-five hours of training, and you'll choose to volunteer from five to fifteen hours a week during the school year.
www.aarp.org/experience-corps

SENIOR CORPS

This network of national service programs provides a listing of opportunities for seniors fifty-five and older to serve as foster grandparents, community volunteers, and role models and mentors to individuals and companies. Senior Corps matches over 200,000 Americans with service opportunities every year.
www.nationalservice.gov/programs/senior-corps

ICOULDBE

Working in New York City's public school system, Adam Aberman was struck by its lack of guidance counselors. Each counselor was responsible for the course selection, career exploration and post-secondary school planning for hundreds of students. How would children, especially first-generation college-bound students, get the support they needed?

Aberman founded iCouldBe to change that with an online mentoring program that's integrated into classrooms. Students choose their mentor from a roster of volunteers, typically a professional working in a career field of interest. One class period per week, students work on e-mentoring activities related to academic success, career exploration and post-secondary educational planning. Mentors commit to one hour a week of online mentoring during the school year. Because the mentoring is done online through electronic messages, and not in real time, mentors can participate any time they can log onto their computers to answer questions, share feedback on their mentees' activities and provide encouragement.

www.icouldbe.org

FOSTER CARE TO SUCCESS (FC2S)

Joseph Rivers had lived in a group home for his entire childhood and knew how difficult it was to turn eighteen and enter the world of adulthood with no caring support system. So in 1981 he founded what is today Foster Care to Success, which matches volunteer mentors with foster youths in college. Mentors make a one-year commitment to communicating at least once a week via phone, text, email or social media. FC2S estimates the time investment at one to three hours a week. Mentors must be twenty-five or older, participate in online training and attend monthly instructional conference calls.

www.fc2success.org

IMERMAN ANGELS

When Jonny Imerman was diagnosed with testicular cancer at age twenty-six, he had never met anyone his age who was a cancer survivor, and he wanted to talk to someone who had faced the same type of cancer. To provide that for others, he founded Imerman Angels. The nonprofit matches people who have cancer with survivors of the same cancer. It also matches caregivers and those who have lost someone to cancer with people who have had the same experience. They try to match people in similar phases of life so that there's a deeper understanding of needs. Imerman Angels has matched people in more than ninety countries with mentors. You can sign up and find or become a mentor through its website. My wife found her Imerman Angel to be an invaluable support.

www.imermanangels.org

TEAM IMPACT

This program connects children facing serious and chronic illness with local college athletic teams, leading to lifelong bonds and life-changing outcomes. Sign your sports team up.

www.goteamimpact.org

LETTERS TO A PRE-SCIENTIST

This program pairs fifth through tenth graders from low-income communities with science, technology, engineering and math (STEM) pen pals. Macon Lowman started this letter-writing program when she was teaching sixth-grade science in rural North Carolina and realized that her students could use inspiration from real world scientists. She teamed up with Anna Goldstein, a scientist who helped to foster a network of STEM professionals to serve as pen pals. Through one-on-one matching, students have the opportunity to ask a real STEM professional questions about college and broaden their awareness of what scientists and technologists do. Teachers facilitate letter exchanges over the school year, and volunteer pen pals can be in science- or technology-related fields or in college. Volunteers register during the summer before the school year and are matched with kids interested in their particular fields.
www.prescientist.org

MENTORING VETERANS THROUGH AMERICAN CORPORATE PARTNERS

American Corporate Partners (ACP) has a mentoring program to help service members, veterans and their spouses build fulfilling careers and bridge the gap between the military and the private sector. Pairs are matched based on career compatibility and interest. Mentors commit to one conversation a month over the course of a year. Topics typically include résumé review, interview preparation, career exploration and advancement, work-life balance and networking. Matches are supported by ACP staff.
www.acp-usa.org

Help People Celebrate

THE CONFETTI FOUNDATION

When Stephanie Frazier Grimm would visit her godson in the hospital, she'd notice that the hospital gave kids a present on their birthdays but that there weren't parties. Recalling her own thirteenth birthday spent in the hospital, she decided to change how hospitalized children celebrate and founded the Confetti Foundation. The foundation delivers a birthday box with handmade birthday cards, party supplies, a toy, a book, crayons, colored pencils and other supplies for kids who are in the hospital or hospice. Families can request one of more than a hundred birthday boxes with themes ranging from Fortnite to unicorns. And when there's a special request, like one family's request for a "camouflage" birthday, they find a way to pull it off. The birthday boxes even include a roll of tape so that families, who often don't leave their sick child's side, can hang up the streamers, banner and decorations. The organization needs volunteers to make birthday cards and birthday banners, and you can also donate $40, which covers the cost of a birthday party.

www.confettifoundation.org

CHEERFUL GIVERS

Robin Zelaya wanted to do more than just write checks to charities without knowing what happened to the money, so she started asking around about nonprofits she should check out. That's when she discovered that a colleague ran a food shelf out of his house. On a child's birthday, parents could get a cake mix or, if there was no cake mix, a box of the child's favorite cereal. Inspired to help, Robin started putting together birthday bags that same week. She took the bags to homeless shelters and food shelves with the requirement that they be given to parents so that they had gifts to give their kids.

Cheerful Givers has distributed more than a million birthday bags in Minnesota since Robin founded the nonprofit in 1993. You can donate $10 to pay for a birthday toy that goes in the bag or follow the directions on the website to create your own bag. You'll need to contact your local shelter or food shelf to ensure that it's interested and to coordinate delivery.

www.cheerfulgivers.org

THE BIRTHDAY PARTY PROJECT

Paige Chenault, a former event planner, was pregnant and thinking about the birthday parties she'd throw for her future child when she opened a copy of *Time* magazine and saw a photograph of a child living in poverty. *What about him?* she thought. *What about kids who won't have birthday parties?* So she started throwing a monthly birthday party for kids at a homeless shelter in Dallas and called it the Birthday Party Project. During the first party, an eleven-year-old approached her and said, "Thank you, Ms. Paige. This is the first birthday party I've ever had." Today, the nonprofit brings birthday parties to shelters in twenty cities. If you live in one of those cities, you can volunteer. Anyone can donate toward the parties, and you can also donate $50 to cover the cost to create and ship a birthday in a bag to social workers who are working with kids in homeless shelters or child protective services. www.thebirthdaypartyproject.org

FOSTER CARE TO SUCCESS (FC2S)

In addition to mentoring, college scholarships and other services, FC2S provides care packages that include cards, cookies, booklets about succeeding in college and gift cards three times a year for foster youths in college. Its Valentine's care package includes a red scarf that volunteers knit or crochet. "It's so critical for the students to know someone cares," Executive Director Eileen McCaffrey says. "We get calls and emails from students all the time about how much the care packages mean to them." A donation of $300 covers the cost of three care packages. www.fc2success.org

THE MOST UP-TO-DATE VERSION OF THE HALL OF FAME CAN BE FOUND ONLINE AT:

www.bradaronson.com/book-resources

ACKNOWLEDGEMENTS

Thank you to . . .

Mia, who supports my crazy ideas and doesn't let the little things slip through the cracks. Her preferred books aren't the "feel-good" kind, but she still read this thoroughly and provided excellent feedback.

Jack and Richard, who provide us with great perspective on life and an abundance of fun times.

Kyndale, who constantly reminds us to be creative, especially when it comes to interesting food combinations.

Alicia, who taught us about BTS and is so much fun to be around.

Our awesome nieces Alex and Kayden.

The countless people who showed my family what it means to be there for someone when life gets hard—really hard. Especially our parents.

Mia's physician Selina Luger and all the nurses at HUP who were incredible. We're forever grateful to you.

The young people I've met and taught over the years. There's nothing more inspiring than spending time with people who have decided to make a change in their lives and then seeing them do it.

The heroes who shared their stories in this book. You're my inspiration.

Doug Wagner and Toni Robino at Windword Literary Services, who were wonderful collaborators through the entire book writing process from concept development to dotting the last "i." Without them I couldn't have done justice to the stories in this book or been comfortable letting go of them. If you need to hire a literary team, these are your people.

LifeTree Media and publisher Maggie Langrick for publishing my book, having patience with me and providing help, guidance and encouragement during the process.

Sarah Brohman, my editor at LifeTree Media, who helped carry this book over the finish line, made smart suggestions about flow and was generous in giving me "one last read" before I finally let go. Copy editor Kate Unrau for her diligence in the details. Publishing coordinator Jesmine Cham who patiently answered all my questions and kept everything moving. Thanks to Morgan Krehbiel for beautiful cover and interior page design, and JoAnne Burek for excellent proofing and indexing.

Suleika Jaouad, who suggested that Mia and I invent projects to keep focused during Mia's treatment. Diving into this book was my project.

My brother, for being the G.O.A.T. and reading so many drafts, and his wife, Tippi.

Lisa Weinert, for her publishing expertise, help and support.

Angela Baka, who helped with the bibliography and other administrative tasks related to the book.

Bob Goff, whose book *Love Does* is one of my all-time favorites and inspired my first chapter.

Eli Schwarz and Louis Cipriano, who interned with me to build a social media following and have adventures in online marketing.

Right before turning in my manuscript I panicked. Does my book suck? Did my writing do justice to the inspiring people I wrote about? Are there sections I should cut? With only a week before deadline, I reached out frantically to some people who generously read this on short notice and provided feedback that improved the book and allowed me to more calmly submit my manuscript. Thank you, Catherine Signorello, Adam Schlossman, Cheryl Rice, Dee Siconolfi and Dan Rhoton! Barry Waldman was also a last-minute help, reading my Hanumas story as he was boarding a plane.

Other readers who contributed their valuable feedback included Cathy Requate, Nate Nichols, Andy Sullivan, Alana Light, Richard Fernandes, Farrah Kennedy, my parents, Wil Reynolds, Carl Tishler, Bart and Erin Hook, Meg Thomson, Ron Spring, Vicki Solot and Pam Iorio. Also, Aparna Mukherjee, who provided input and early edits.

For reading the book and giving me great advice about the business of selling books, thank you Kevin Kruse and Andrea Lavinthal. For advice about the process, thank you Gabriel Weinberg, Dale Atkins, Amanda Salzhauer, Laura Schroff and Lexy Bloom. Thanks to Ron Nordmann for helping me out at the last minute. Also, thanks Bart Hook for excellent web and graphic design work.

And thank *you* for reading this book and all the good you're going to do in the world.

(I had been working on a business book when I decided to focus on *HumanKind* instead, and I'd like to take this opportunity to also thank the folks who took the time to help with that project. For your thorough reads and excellent feedback, thank you Rich Sedmak, Steve Roth, Noel Weyrich, John Avondolio, my parents and in-laws, Anthony Pisapia, Kevin Nalty and Chris Schroeder, whose advice has significantly improved my writing.)

NOTES

....

1   Donna McGuire, *Santa's Secret: A Story of Hope* (Lee's Summit, Missouri: World 2 Publishing, 2007).

2   Jim Abbott, *Imperfect: An Improbable Life* (New York: Ballantine Books, 2013).

3   Nunu's quotes were provided by the Himalayan Cataract Project (www.cureblindness.org).

4   Note on the HCP calculations: In 2018, HCP provided 123,648 sight-saving surgeries. From 80 to 90 percent of those surgeries were cataract surgeries to cure blindness, so I used 85 percent for my calculations. Some people require cataract surgery on both eyes, which would count as two surgeries. If it's assumed that every person needed surgery for both eyes and 85 percent of the surgeries were cataract surgeries, the cost per person cured of blindness would be about $195. This also assumes that HCP's entire budget is spent on surgeries when they also funded eye exams and basic eye care for nearly 1.7 million people and trained physicians who will provide life-changing eye surgeries at no cost to HCP. So $195 is probably a high estimate of the cost. HCP reports the cost of materials for one sight-restoring surgery at $25.

5   Julie's and Sandy's quotations were provided by You Matter Marathon.

6   Helen Mrosla's idea first appeared in *Proteus: A Journal of Ideas* (Shippensburg, PA: Shippensburg University, 1991) as quoted in Jack Canfield and Mark Victor Hansen, *Chicken Soup for the Teacher's Soul* (Cos Cob, CT: Chicken Soup for the Soul Publishing, 2012).

7   Mariel Alper, Joshua Markman, and Matthew R. Durose, "2018 Update on Prisoner Recidivism: A 9-Year Follow-up Period (2005–2014)" (Report, US Department of Justice, Office of Justice Programs, Bureau of Justice Statistics, May 2018), 1, www.bjs.gov/content/pub/pdf/18upr9yfup0514.pdf.

8   Jack Andraka, "A promising test for pancreatic cancer . . . from a teenager" (Filmed February 2013 at Long Beach, CA. TED video, 10:37) www.ted.com /talks/jack_andraka_a_promising_test_for_pancreatic_cancer_from_a _teenager/.

9   Karen was on medication that affected her memory at the time and can't recall the aide's name.

10   J. Fuller, M. Raman, et al, *Dismissed by Degrees* (Report. Boston: Accenture, Grads of Life, Harvard Business School, October 2017).

    Amanda Beddingfield, ed., *Employer Playbook* (Arlington, VA: CEB Global (now Gartner), 2015), gradsoflife.org/wp-content/uploads/2017/06/2015 -09-18-Tech-Hire_EmployerPlaybook.pdf.

11   Jean Baldwin Grossman, Joseph P. Tierney, and Nancy Resch, "Making a Difference: An Impact Study of Big Brothers Big Sisters" (Reissue of 1995 Study. Philadelphia, PA: Public Private Ventures, 2000), 30.

12   Big Brothers Big Sisters, "Adult Little Research." (Rochester, NY: Harris Interactive, March 3 to April 16, 2009), 6.

13   Sanford Greenberg, "The Judgment of Solomon" (Presentation at the Lasker/International Retinal Research Foundation Initiative's plenary session "Restoring Vision to the Blind," Janelia Farm, Ashburn, VA, March 2014), webvision.med.utah.edu/2014/05/the-judgement-of-solomon/.

14   Shawn Achor, *The Happiness Advantage: How a Positive Brain Fuels Success in Work and Life* (New York: Currency, 2010), 15, 45–48.

15   Robert Emmons, *Thanks!: How The New Science of Gratitude Can Make You Happier* (New York: Houghton Mifflin Harcourt, 2007), 27–35, 47–48.

16   Michael F. Steger, Todd B. Kashdan, and Shigehiro Oishi, "Being good by doing good: Daily eudaimonic activity and well-being," *Journal of Research in Personality*, 42 (2008): 22–42.

17   The idea for this exercise came from a post by Dave Frees at Successtechnologies.com.

18   Alisha Coleman-Jensen, et al, "Household Food Security in the United States in 2017" (United States Department of Agriculture, Economic Research Service, September 2018), 9.

    Ellen L. Bassuk, et al, "America's Youngest Outcasts A Report Card on Child Homelessness" (American Institutes for Research, The National Center on Family Homelessness, November 2014), 6.

    Economic Mobility Project and Public Safety Performance Project, "Collateral Costs: Incarceration's Effect on Economic Mobility" (Washington, DC: The Pew Charitable Trusts, 2010), 4.

19   See note 4.

20   Julia B. Isaacs, "Starting School at a Disadvantage: The School Readiness of Poor Children" (March 19, 2012) 2, www.brookings.edu/research /starting-school-at-a-disadvantage-the-school-readiness-of-poor-children/.

The Children's Reading Foundation, "Predicting and Preventing Student Failure: What You Can Do to Ensure Students Succeed!" (Kennewick, WA: The Children's Reading Foundation, 2015), 2–3, www.readingfoundation.org/axmag/Predicting_and_Preventing_Student _Failure/FLASH/index.html.

BIBLIOGRAPHY

BOOKS

Abbott, Jim. *Imperfect: An Improbable Life*. New York: Ballantine Books, 2013.

Achor, Shawn. *The Happiness Advantage: How a Positive Brain Fuels Success in Work and Life*. New York: Currency, 2010.

Barbash, Tom. *On Top of the World: Cantor Fitzgerald, Howard Lutnick, and 9/11: A Story of Loss and Renewal*. New York: Harper Paperbacks, 2003.

Canfield, Jack, and Mark Victor Hansen. *Chicken Soup for the Teacher's Soul*. Cos Cob, CT: Chicken Soup for the Soul Publishing, 2012.

Emmons, Robert. *Thanks!: How the New Science of Gratitude Can Make You Happier*. New York: Houghton Mifflin Harcourt, 2007.

Goff, Bob. *Love Does: Discover a Secretly Incredible Life in an Ordinary World*. Nashville, Tennessee: Thomas Nelson, 2012.

Kristof, Nicholas and Sheryl WuDunn. *A Path Appears: Transforming Lives, Creating Opportunity*. New York: Alfred A. Knopf, 2014.

McGuire, Donna. *Santa's Secret: A Story of Hope*. Lee's Summit, Missouri: World 2 Publishing, 2007.

Relin, David Oliver. *Second Suns: Two Trailblazing Doctors and Their Quest to Cure Blindness, One Pair of Eyes at a Time*. New York: The Experiment, 2016.

Schroff, Laura. *An Invisible Thread: The True Story of an 11-Year-Old Panhandler, a Busy Sales Executive, and an Unlikely Meeting with Destiny*, New York: Howard Books, 2012.

Wayne, Jimmy. *Walk to Beautiful: The Power of Love and a Homeless Kid Who Found the Way*. Nashville, Tennessee: Thomas Nelson, 2015.

TALKS

Andraka, Jack. "A promising test for pancreatic cancer . . . from a teenager." Filmed February 2013 at Long Beach, CA. TED video, 10:37. www.ted.com /talks/jack_andraka_a_promising_test_for_pancreatic_cancer_from_a _teenager/.

Greenberg, Sanford. "The Judgment of Solomon." Presentation at the Lasker/
International Retinal Research Foundation Initiative's plenary session
"Restoring Vision to the Blind," Janelia Farm, Ashburn, VA, March 2014.
webvision.med.utah.edu/2014/05/the-judgement-of-solomon/

Lutnick, Howard. Presentation at Haverford College Family & Friends Weekend,
Haverford, PA, October 2011. www.vidinfo.org/video/2179318/howard
-lutnick-83-at-haverford-college-family.

STAND-ALONE RESEARCH STUDIES, WHITE PAPERS

Alper, Mariel, Matthew R. Durose, and Joshua Markman. "2018 Update on Prisoner Recidivism: A 9-Year Follow-up Period (2005–2014)." Report. Washington: U.S. Department of Justice, Office of Justice Programs, Bureau of Justice
Statistics, May 2018. www.bjs.gov/content/pub/pdf/18upr9yfup0514.pdf.

Bassuk, Ellen L., Carmela J. DeCandia, Corey Anne Beach, and Fred Berman.
"America's Youngest Outcasts A Report Card on Child Homelessness."
Waltham, MA: American Institutes for Research, The National Center on
Family Homelessness, November 2014. www.air.org/sites/default/files
/downloads/report/Americas-Youngest-Outcasts-Child-Homelessness
-Nov2014.pdf.

Beddingfield, Amanda, ed. *Employer Playbook: Best Practices and Tools to Recruit
Technology Talent from Nontraditional Sources.* Arlington, VA: CEB Global (now
Gartner), 2015. gradsoflife.org/wp-content/uploads/2017/06/2015-09-18
-Tech-Hire_EmployerPlaybook.pdf.

Big Brothers Big Sisters. "Adult Little Research." Rochester, NY: Harris
Interactive, March 3 to April 16, 2009.

The Children's Reading Foundation. "Predicting and Preventing Student
Failure: What You Can Do to Ensure Students Succeed!" Kennewick, WA:
The Children's Reading Foundation, 2015. www.readingfoundation.org
/axmag/Predicting_and_Preventing_Student_Failure/FLASH/index.html.

Coleman-Jensen, Alisha, Matthew P. Rabbitt, Christian A. Gregory, and Anita
Singh. "Household Food Security in the United States in 2017, ERR-256."
Washington: U.S. Department of Agriculture, Economic Research Service,
2018. www.ers.usda.gov/webdocs/publications/90023/err-256.pdf.

Economic Mobility Project and Public Safety Performance Project. "Collateral
Costs: Incarceration's Effect on Economic Mobility." Washington, DC: The
Pew Charitable Trusts, 2010. www.pewtrusts.org/~/media/legacy
/uploadedfiles/pcs_assets/2010/collateralcosts1pdf.pdf.

Fuller, J., M. Raman, et al. *Dismissed by Degrees: How degree inflation is under-
mining U.S. competitiveness and hurting America's middle class.* Report. Boston:
Accenture, Grads of Life, Harvard Business School, October 2017.

Isaacs, Julia B. "Starting School at a Disadvantage: The School Readiness of Poor Children." March 19, 2012. www.brookings.edu/research/starting -school-at-a-disadvantage-the-school-readiness-of-poor-children/.

Lattice. *Working It Out: Real people tell true stories about the moments that changed their career.* San Francisco, CA: Lattice. Accessed October 2019. lattice.com/library/working-it-out.

Tierney, Joseph P., Jean Baldwin Grossman, and Nancy L Resch. "Making a Difference: An Impact Study of Big Brothers Big Sisters." Reissue of 1995 Study. Philadelphia, PA: Public Private Ventures, 2000.

JOURNALS AND PERIODICALS

Mullen, Mike. "Coon Rapids mosque gets touching 'thank you' note from unknown neighbors." *City Pages*, February 7, 2017. www.citypages.com/news /coon-rapids-mosque-gets-touching-thank-you-note-from-unknown -neighbors/413013393.

Poulin, Michael J., Stephanie L. Brown, Amanda J. Dillard, and Dylan M. Smith. "Giving to Others and the Association Between Stress and Mortality." *American Journal of Public Health* 103, no. 9 (September 1, 2013): 1649–1655.

Steger, Michael F., Todd B. Kashdan, and Shigehiro Oishi. "Being Good by Doing Good: Daily Eudaimonic Activity and Well-Being." *Journal of Research in Personality*, 42 (2008): 22–42.

FILM, TV AND RADIO

Andraka, Jack. "Boy Wonder." Interview by Morley Safer. *60 Minutes*, CBS, October 13, 2013. Video, 13.36. www.cbsnews.com/news/boy-wonder -jack-andraka/.

Arnold, Jennifer, dir. *A Small Act.* 2010. Harambee Media and HBO Documentary Films. DVD.

Chapman, Bev. "Blessed: The Story of KC's Secret Santa." KMBC 9. November 11, 2007. YouTube video, 6:28. www.youtube.com/watch?v =xp7q6OHKTbA&list=PLCF345CF0B31D070C&index=3.

Ramsey, David. *Dave Ramsey Show.* December 11, 2006. cdn.ramseysolutions .net/media/3_way_universal/christmas/audio/chr09_Secret_Santa _12112006.mp3.

WEBSITES

Altucher, James. "Five Things I Learned from Superman." Thought Catalog. Published August 5, 2013. thoughtcatalog.com/james-altucher/2013/08 /5things-i-learned-from-superman/.

CASA of Southeast Texas. "Ryan Dollinger: CASA Is My Lifesaver." Posted to Facebook October 3, 2018. www.facebook.com/CumberlandCountyCASA /posts/2006834492709237/.

Forbes. "UFC President Dana White Explains His Change Of Heart On Nick Newell." Posted June 12, 2018. www.forbes.com/sites/trentreinsmith/2018 /06/12/ufc-president-dana-white-explains-his-change-of-heart-on-nick -newell/#8abfd3430832.

The Jewish Chronicle. "Why an 88-year-old Holocaust survivor has become a heroine to young Africans." Published April 21, 2011. www.thejc.com /culture/film/why-an-88-year-old-holocaust-survivor-has-become-a-heroine -to-young-africans-1.68510.

Movies that Matter NL. "Portrait Chris Mburu and Hilde Back." Filmed 2011. Video. www.moviesthatmatter.nl/festival/archief/archief_2011 /portretten_activisten_2011.

Psychology Today. "Helper's High: The Benefits (and Risks) of Altruism." Published September 4, 2014. www.psychologytoday.com/us/blog /high-octane-women/201409/helpers-high-the-benefits-and-risks-altruism.

Redditt. "To the lady at Trader Joe's who almost made me cry . . . thank you." January 31, 2018. www.reddit.com/r/TwoXChromosomes/comments/7uf53x /to_the_lady_at_trader_joes_who_almost_made_me_cry/.

Rolling Stone. "Jimmy Wayne Talks True 'Paper Angels' Story That Inspired New Movie." Published November 14, 2014. www.rollingstone.com/music /music-country/jimmy-wayne-talks-true-paper-angels-story-that-inspired -new-movie-241019/.

Success Technologies, Inc. "You Get What You Look For! Why That's True and What to Do About It." Published May 2010. www.successtechnologies.com /2010/05/you-get-what-you-look-for-why-thats-true-and-what-to-do-about-it/.

Upworthy. "A viral post helps explain what to say—and what not to say—to a parent who has lost a child." Posted July 12, 2019. www.upworthy.com /parent-child-death-what-not-to-say.

U.S. Department of Health and Human Services, Health Resources & Services Administration. "The Need for More Marrow Donors." Accessed June 6, 2019. bloodcell.transplant.hrsa.gov/donor/need_for_donors/index.html.

YouTube. "A Small Act." Published on March 28, 2011. www.youtube.com/watch ?v=a4q_QPEnGcg&t=3s.

YouTube. "Salad Days" from Giving You the Business (S1, E9). youtu.be/o2 -Cz3prfz8.

RECOMMENDED READING
AND VIEWING

....

IF YOU LIKED THIS BOOK, I think you'll also like these. I read and watched these inspiring books and videos for background for some of my stories.

An Invisible Thread: The True Story of an 11-Year-Old Panhandler, a Busy Sales Executive, and an Unlikely Meeting with Destiny, Laura Schroff's story about meeting eleven-year-old Maurice and building a lifelong relationship over lunch (Howard Books, 2012)

A Small Act, Jennifer Arnold's documentary about Hilde Back's "small" act of kindness (Harambee Media and HBO Documentary Films, 2010)

Love Does: Discover a Secretly Incredible Life in an Ordinary World, Bob Goff's book about his life. I enjoyed this book and his message so much that I used the title for my first chapter (Thomas Nelson, 2012)

Imperfect: An Improbable Life, Jim Abbott's memoir about his life (Ballantine Books, 2013)

Santa's Secret: A Story of Hope, Donna McGuire's book about Secret Santa Larry Stewart (World 2 Publishing, 2007)

Second Suns: Two Trailblazing Doctors and Their Quest to Cure Blindness, One Pair of Eyes at a Time, David Oliver Relin's story of two doctors who founded Himalayan Cataract Project (The Experiment, 2016)

Walk to Beautiful: The Power of Love and a Homeless Kid Who Found the Way, Jimmy Wayne's story of life as a homeless kid who found his way (and the life-changing guitar he received through the Angel Tree Program) (Thomas Nelson, 2015)

Jack Andraka's TED Talk about his efforts to develop a better diagnostic test for pancreatic cancer. The URL is quite long, but you can do a Google search or go to bradaronson.com/book-resources to get a direct link.

The Happiness Advantage: How a Positive Brain Fuels Success in Work and Life. Shawn Achor's book has information about how we can make ourselves happier. It goes well with the recommendations I provided in Chapter 8 about changing perspective (Currency, 2010)

A Path Appears: Transforming Lives, Creating Opportunity, Nicholas Kristof and Sheryl WuDunn. A book with suggestions on how we can make a difference in the world (Alfred A. Knopf, 2014)

Christmas Jars, Jason F. Wright, a feel-good novel about the spirit of Christmas (Shadow Mountains, 2005)

INDEX

················

A

A Small Act (documentary), 52, 53, 54

Abbott, Jim (Jimmy), 47–50, 51

Aberman, Adam, 220

Achieving Independence Center (AIC), 147–148

acknowledgement and appreciation, 20, 60, 61–62, 90–93, 95–97, 176, 177

acts of kindness

  daily opportunities, 157

  and drop-in-the-bucket thinking, 15

  getting started, 195

  paying it forward movement, 192–194

  to pedestrians, 40

  for people going through a rough time, 20–23

  working into schedules, 73–76

  see also caring; communities; conversations; donations and gifts; holiday support; inclusiveness; letter-writing; philanthropy

AdvisorNet, 218

Ahmad, Adeel, 22–23

AIC *see* Achieving Independence Center (AIC)

Aid for Friends, 180, 181

Aljalian, Natasha and Gabriel, 136–142

Altucher, James, 5

Alzheimer's disease *see* dementia

Amachi, 186–187, 194

American Corporate Partners, 218

An Invisible Thread (Schroff), 28, 31

Andraka, Jack, 104–106

Andrea (Brad's cousin), 8

Angel Tree program, 190–192, 204

Anthony (food delivery recipient), 182

Any Refugee, 213

Any Soldier, 216–217

aQuantive, 120–122

Aronson, Brad

  and forgotten wallet, 43–45

  and Jack, 135–136

  and Mia's treatments, 18–19

  and Nanny, 55–56

  perspective with students, 147–149

  and Popop, 120–122

  reacts to Mia's diagnosis, 5–6

  receives help, 6–11, 63–65, 115–116, 200–202

  on receiving feedback, 155–156

  at Ronald McDonald Camp, 159–160, 175–176

  wig fashion show, 177

Aronson, Jack (Brad's son), 6, 7, 135–136, 202

Aronson, Joe (Brad's father), 38

Aronson, Mia (Brad's wife)

  on attitude to chores, 156

  battle with leukemia, 5–8, 18, 64–65, 202

  hospital experiences, 21–22, 77

  "Mia Appreciation Day", 176

  thoughtfulness of, 44, 60

Aronson, Rob (Brad's brother), 6–7, 76–77, 106–107, 174

Aronson family

  Hanumas tradition, 172–175

  and mentorship, 131–132, 133

  see also Nanny (Brad's grandmother); Popop (Brad's grandfather)

Art (Sandy Greenberg's roommate), 153–154, 155

autism, 11–12, 14, 95, 112

239

CPSIA information can be obtained
at www.ICGtesting.com
Printed in the USA
BVHW040220131222
654108BV00004B/234

9 781928 055631